*Charli
May this book
affirm your belief in*

"A spiritual, provocative book. Josiane, a true vision-
ary, speaks from her direct experience in a way that
heals the soul." **Ron Valle, PhD, Author,**
*Phenomenological Inquiry: Existential
& Transpersonal Dimensions*

Heaven, Lae Carol

"Fascinating and inspiring reading. Josiane traces her
spirituality from her childhood in France to the United
States, and her ongoing work as a bridge between
cultures and dimensions. I have known Cedar Woman
for many moons, and honor and respect her work."
Walking Eagle, Karuk spiritual leader

"Profound and insightful. *Whispers of the Soul*
describes Josiane's search for wholeness that can
transform readers and offers them a better understanding of their own unique journey through life."
**Dr. Stanley Krippner, Saybrook Institute
San Francisco**

D1478361

Whispers of the Soul

Journeys to the Other Side of Life

Josiane Antonette

Library of Congress Catalog Card Number: 98-092955
Antonette, Josiane, 1942-

ISBN 0-9664552-9-0

Some of the people's names in the book have been changed to protect their identities.

Editorial: Shahan Jon and Dana Conant

Cover Photo of Black Butte, Mt. Shasta, CA: ©1986 Josiane Antonette
(This is an original, unaltered photograph.)

Cover Design: Arthur Miller

Page Design: Quicksilver Productions, Mt. Shasta, CA

Dedication

This book is dedicated to my children,

Jean Pierre, Philippe and Aydee,

and to my grandchildren.

May they listen to the whispers of their souls,

and know how beautiful they truly are.

Prologue

For as long as I can remember, I never simply accepted anything I was told without first questioning it. I believed only what I had personally experienced. But I have a story to tell you. My story might be your story; incredible, yet true.

This story is my very personal journey to wholeness which I humbly and respectfully share with you. As you read it, may you hear the whispers of your soul, remember how beautiful you really are, and express this beauty by embracing life passionately. May it inspire, delight, and contribute understanding of your own living and dying and that of your loved ones.

My journey started fifty-six years ago with my grandmother in Corsica (France) where I experienced my first glimpses of the other side of life, the world of spirit. I did not know that later this would become my passion, the subject of a long journey of investigation into the realm of the unseen, and eventually a way of life. Communication with spirit has always occupied a major place in my life, consciously or in the dream time. Following my calling was a painful process for me, as well as for those who were not ready to see me in my wholeness. Despite my understanding of their need to keep me the way they wanted me to be, I had no choice but to search for the meaning of my own life.

I have traveled the perilous journey between the mundane world and the world of spirit many times; now I feel at home in both. After a near-death experience in my early twenties, I no longer feared death and made peace with my life on earth as well. As the result of all my experiences, I serve as a bridge between the two sides of life in a process I call "Awakening the Soul," assisting individuals in their search to remember—to fully embrace their unique spirituality. I help them meet their own higher guidance, the voice of their soul. I also offer myself as a medium to contact their departed loved ones if there is a need for healing in those relationships. With assistance from my own higher guidance, I facilitate the healing of body and soul. For more than thirty years, I have worked with the dying and the living: in hospitals as a chaplain, universities as a teacher, as a spiritual counselor, healer and ceremonial leader. My understanding of living, dying, and the spiritual realms has touched many people.

My own learning deepens each day as I experience new possibilities for growth and wholeness. My connection with spirit fills my life with wonder and great joy, and inspires me to create new programs which support spirituality in the world. I live a life based upon my visions and my own truth, bridging heaven and earth, walking gently upon the planet, and singing passionately my love song to the Creator. I pray that as you read this book, you will be compelled to heal your life according to your own unique vision of yourself. In some way, may this book serve your experience of heaven on earth.

Josiane Antonette
Mt. Shasta, California
February 1998

Table of Contents

Only passion, great passion
can elevate the soul to great things.

Denis Diderot

Acknowledgements

I would first like to acknowledge…

…all the teachers in the physical world and the world of spirit whom the Creator has sent into my life throughout the years, and who taught me to listen to my soul…

…my patients who blessed me by sharing the most intimate time of their lives—their "death"—and for trusting my abilities to direct them to the other side of life…

…my parents Charles and Jeanne who brought me to this country so I could fulfill my destiny…

…my grandmother from whom I learned the meaning of unconditional love…

My deepest thanks to all who have helped me in writing this book, and supported me in good and bad times…

…my special heartfelt thanks to my son, Jean Pierre Moser, who made my dream of thirty years possible by financially supporting the creation of this book, and for the faith he had in me…

…to my partner Arthur Miller, for his unquestioning support and encouragement…

…to my adopted daughter and first editor, Christine Guaulin…

...to my editor Shahan Jon for her patience, guidance and expertise, and the long hours she spent correcting my Anglo/French writing skills...

...to Dr. Stanley Krippner for taking time in his busy schedule to review my manuscript, for his gentle suggestions and well-informed corrections...

...to Dr. John Miller for his mastery of the English language, and for his encouraging me to share more of myself...

...to the Miller family for their loving support and trust in my abilities...

...to Marion Miller for supporting me in publishing this book...

...to Pat Miller and Jeannine Garrison for doing the last review of the book...

I have been blessed beyond words...

Love is the emblem of eternity,
it confounds all notion of time,
effaces all memory of a beginning,
all fear of an end.

Madame De Staël

CHAPTER ONE

Mémé

I was three weeks old when my parents sent me to Corsica in the icy spring of 1942. The world was at war, and the Allies were raiding the cities and seas in their effort to protect France from the invaders. My Uncle Antoine and my grandmother came to pick me up in the seaport of Marseille, France, where my family lived at that time, and we set upon our dangerous journey. My uncle attached tires to my bed while we sailed to the island home of my ancestors so if we met with mishap, my bed would float and I would have a chance to be saved. They always told me the story of how I was the "Little Moses."

Corsica is an island in the Mediterranean Sea south of France which had been an important junction for the commercial routes of antiquity. In Arabic, the island's name means 'Seat of God,' but it was once named 'Kaliste' in honor of the Greek priestess Artemis—the huntress who stands with the wolf—Goddess of the Moon. The Corsicans love their island with deep passion, and believe without question that it is the center of earth.

Mémé Raphaëlla

Corsica, 1944. Josiane standing in front of the statue of Napoleon.

As a young girl, Corsica meant Grandmother's home to me—my home—where the smell of coffee brewing on the stove woke me in the morning, and I was greeted with smiles which told me I was loved. My nights were filled with the scent of fresh bread baking in the bakery on the first floor of our building mixed with the fresh sea breeze. I fell asleep watching the flickering candlelight creating dancing shadows on the walls and ceiling. In the morning, Grandmother and I went to the market to buy fresh produce for the day. On our way we always stopped at the port to see my grandfather, uncle and cousins who were fishermen. We usually found them mending their fishing nets for their next trip and singing old, melodic Corsican songs. Corsica was my universe, my playground.

In the summer, I ran barefoot through the streets to the beach, free as a wild goat, returning home only when I was hungry and leaving again to play until dinner. After dinner in the summer evenings, if the young adults did not take us children with them on their "promenade"— a stroll to the plaza in the center of town to meet with their friends—the family gathered on the balcony to enjoy the cool sea breeze and talk late into the night. During the rainy winter nights, the whole extended family, including uncles, cousins and neighbors, gathered around the fireplace in the kitchen and told stories. Pépé, my grandfather, had traveled all over the world on a great sailing ship. I was fascinated by his stories of leaving home at fourteen to join the Merchant Marines, his adventures through the rough seas in the Straits of Magellan, and visits to exotic places like the Dead Sea.

Our home was situated in the old part of town in the building where Napoleon Bonaparte had been born. I used to play in the courtyard where he played as a boy, and many times pretended I was he. All of the houses were built in a circle with Napoleon's home in the center. From our balcony we could see all the other families in this close community. By the light of the summer moon, community members gathered on their balconies, exchanged stories, and even welcomed one another's guests.

We had a very hard time obtaining the basic necessities in Corsica during the war because the island was cut off from the mainland. Many went without food for long periods. But one thing was never lacking: the loving support of older children and adults, family members and neighbors acting as surrogate mothers and fathers. There was a strong feeling of community. Everyone helped rear children and take care of the sick, the dying, and the elderly.

Mémé, my grandmother, was a member of a Corsican lineage of women who were healers. The *Sage Femme* (sage women) were those who protected home and animals with their prayers and who healed everyone. These women of wisdom were always older than fifty, when it was assumed a woman had completed the responsibility of child rearing and could dedicate herself to her community.

Mémé was known as "Zia" Raphaëlla. Only a woman, who proved by her lifelong dedication to her spiritual work and the people, had the great honor of being called "Zia," or Aunt. But to me as a child growing up in Corsica, she was simply "Mémé," Grandmother. I remember not understanding why she was called "Zia," and it even bothered me that she could be everybody's aunt. Later, when I started to make sense of my childhood, I came to realize how I had been blessed with the great opportunity to be part of her life and the oral tradition passed on from woman to woman for thousands of years. Although, with the coming of Catholicism, the old tradition incorporated Mother Mary, Jesus, Joseph, and, of course, the various saints, the old tradition was practiced all the same.

Mémé was an "Incantatora"—a woman who knew the oral tradition of specific native prayers for the living, the dying, and the departed ones. She could also interpret dreams and omens and see into the future.

One time, I was brought to a "Signatora"—a woman whose trade was to heal physical illness and, through the use of oil, to offer clairvoyant consultation. I was ill, and Mémé wanted to consult her old friend the "Signatora" Zia Louisa.

Zia Louisa's home was located on the third floor of an old stone building. As we climbed the high stairs, I was nervous. We children called the healer a "matzera," a witch.

We knocked on the door. When the "Signatora" came to greet us, I thought I was going to faint with fear! She was dressed all in black. Her long skirt touched the floor, and I could not see her feet. Her arms were covered by a long shawl, white hair held by a scarf. The only thing I could focus on were her small, dark, deep-set eyes. They seemed to gaze right through me. I felt that I was never going to leave this place alive if I didn't hang on to Grandmother's hand!

With a stern look, the "Signatora" motioned for me to get closer to a table in the middle of the room. Mémé gave me a gentle push. I had to let go of her hand!

Two candles stood on the table covered by a white cloth. One was placed in the north and the other in the south. In the center of the table, a plate held water, and to its right were a bottle of olive oil and a small bowl.

Zia Louisa approached the table, poured the oil into the bowl, and raised it. As she began her incantations, she moved the bowl in a clockwise circular motion around my head. Then she poured three drops of oil into the water and asked me to look in the center of the plate.

I could see the oil taking different shapes and moving closer together to become one big smear.

The Signatora's prayers in the native language grew louder and louder. Then she took a pair of scissors, held the blades above a lighted candle, and dipped them into the water while cutting the oil. The smear separated, and drops of oil dispersed in many directions.

The ritual was over. Mémé and Zia whispered as they looked at me, and their hands made animated gestures. I never knew what they talked about, but the next day I felt better, and the next, even better.

Another time I accompanied Mémé when she went to assist a "Sfumatora"—the one who makes smoke. Her trade was to heal by invoking spirit helpers and the afterlife through the burning of herbs gathered at different times of the year in the "Maquis," the desert hills surrounding the city of Ajaccio. When we arrived, I was asked to play with the other children outside, but I was very curious. The door was left open and I peeked in, making myself invisible. All the window blinders were closed, and the room was dark for such a bright summer afternoon. As my eyes adjusted to the dim light, I saw a group of women chanting incantations as they burned various herbs in a small cast iron cauldron filled with red-hot coals. The woman in charge of the ritual was dressed all in black, similar to many of the older women. I was breathless. I knew that one simple look from "zia" would bring a curse on me! I was scared, but I could feel something powerful and sacred all around me. On our way home, I asked Mémé what happened inside the house. "It's not for you to know yet," she responded, "someday maybe, *s'il plait a Dieu*— if it pleases God."

There were other aspects of the trade, too. The "Tundra" was the one who could heal at a distance. "La Mammana" practiced midwifery. Most women practiced a combination of all the different ways of the trade, using herbs, clairvoyance, communication with the afterlife and spirits, and dream interpretation. Not all practiced midwifery, and the midwife did not always practice the rest of the trade. To this day, the incantations, prayers and evocations are being used in the Corsican native language as taught in the oral tradition passed on from woman to woman.

I slept with Grandmother in the room which had been the chapel of Napoleon's guards' house. The room was filled with history, and Mémé, who was very devout, had religious pictures on every wall. We slept with lighted votive

Corsican child dressed as his parents' favorite saint.

candles all night to "protect the house from evil spirits," she said, "and to show the departed ones their way home" in case they were lost.

On the top of a dresser was a beautiful statue of baby Jesus held in a glass container. He had blue porcelain eyes and curly hair, and wore a white lace robe. I was fascinated and totally in love with the purity and kindness coming from his face. I spent long periods lost in a dream state while gazing at him. Sometimes I asked Grandmother if, when I grew up, it could be mine. She would reply, "When I die, it will be yours."

I remember being surrounded by great passion for the saints. Some of the school children even dressed as specific saints! Their parents had promised saints they would clothe their child in a certain way for so many months, in return for healing the child or a member of the family. There was a seven-year-old boy dressed in an ankle-length brown robe with a rope around his waist in respect for Saint Francis. Another child wore a mutton robe in honor of St. John the Baptist. A young girl wore the sister habit of St. Theresa. Despite their odd appearance, no one ever made fun of these children; to do so would bring bad luck. Each of these children embodied the saint who had been called upon, and they had special privileges in the community. They were part of religious ceremonies, processions in the City, and public prayer.

The "Catinaccio" was held each Easter. This ceremony enacted the passion of Jesus. Men who had something to ask of God were dressed in red robes and hoods and carried heavy wooden crosses barefoot for miles with chains around their ankles. They offered their suffering, blood, and self-flagellation in exchange for forgiveness, or the healing of a loved one, town, or nation, or simply to show total submission to the will of God. Women followed the procession and prayed; some walked on their knees to ask favors of God.

Once I asked Mémé, "Why do people need to hurt themselves in order to be forgiven by God? Who is this God who asks such a thing from his children?"

"It is blasphemy," Mémé answered, "to talk about God in such a manner." She looked around nervously to see if anyone had heard me. "People have choices, and these men need to do what they do, not for God, but for themselves to relieve their suffering and, perhaps, that of a loved one. It is not for you to judge," she added.

Sometimes it seemed that Mémé was talking to herself. When I asked her what she was doing, she simply answered, "I am talking with God."

To Mémé, spirit was part of our everyday life. She applied this belief in a ritualistic way to everything, including the bread we ate in the morning and the soup which warmed our bodies in the evening. Everything that created the food we ate was part of God, and she reminded us how thankful we all should be.

Once, at the end of summer, the women of the family and two neighbors left early in the morning for the market place. They returned carrying bags of tomatoes. Mémé had prepared coffee and rolls for everybody, and then the work began. Each tomato was sliced with precision as everyone laughed, talked, and shared stories. After a long time, when all the tomatoes were sliced, each fruit was gently laid in an orderly arrangement on the rooftop, and prayers were said to keep the rain away for a few days so the tomatoes could dry and bless the wintertime with the full flavor of summer.

That night, everyone was tired but unable to sleep because of the heat. The whole family gathered outside on the ter-race to enjoy the cool sea breeze and conversation. There was no moon; it was difficult to see even the neighboring balconies. We all noticed how dark it was when suddenly we saw a square of light on the wall separating Napoleon's house from the guard residence. The light seemed to be shining from the third floor tenant's window onto the wall. We looked to see who might be there, but there was no light in the apartment. The tenant had gone to a nearby village earlier that day, and had not returned.

When I looked back at the wall, I shivered with cold. My companions and I saw two hands waving back and forth. We stared in wonder.

The next morning while I was still in bed, I heard people murmuring and knew the hushed voices meant someone had died. I later learned that the third-floor apartment tenant had died of a heart attack the night before as we had been sitting on the terrace observing the apparition on the wall. Grandmother explained that the waving hands we had seen in the light on the wall had been our neigh-bor waving good-bye to all of us. He came to his house because, Grandmother explained, "when you die you go to the place you are familiar with." So he had come, looked around, and motioned his good-bye. It was scary to know that our neighbor had come to see us this way. Yet I knew it was possible because I had seen it!

Childhood experiences such as this made me recognize the existence of different levels of reality. As a result, I was enabled later in life to bridge easily the physical world with the world of spirit.

There was no mystery that the dead were part of us. We celebrated the Day of the Dead on the first of November every year with a big feast.

The night before the celebration, the women loaded the tables with all sorts of food they had prepared. There was goat meat prepared in a variety of ways—roasted or stewed—and every part of the body was used; and there were delicious Corsican pastries filled with goat cheese and the essence of orange flowers, and one made with chestnut flour which I adored. We children were not allowed to go to the wake with the adults, and the food, we were told, was for the dead.

How scared we were, and how curious at the same time! I remember trying to look through the lock of the bedroom door to catch a glimpse of a dead spirit. But I was young, and I was never able to stay awake long enough.

The following day there would be no food in sight, so we children really believed the dead came and ate everything! That day, the women and girls would go to the cemetery.

CHAPTER ONE

We would take our brooms and clean up the graves: take the bones and ashes and make room for the time when the grave would be needed for another member of the family. We would eat lunch at the cemetery—the delicious leftovers from the wake—and pray. In this way, the women took care of the dead.

It was natural for me to go to the cemetery, often with the women of the family. I played there. I ate lunch there. I prayed and fashioned little bouquets with the beaded flowers that were made for funerals. Sometimes I would take these flowers home, but Mémé said it was bad luck, and I must return them to the cemetery; they belonged to the dead, not the living. In such daily rituals, I learned to pay respect to the spirits of my ancestors.

As a little girl, I followed Mémé like a shadow. I absorbed everything Grandmother did. My life was exciting and rich; I was thrilled to be alive. Then something happened. It was over.

Our house burned down, and my whole life changed. I remember the smoke, loud shouts in the night, people crying, "Our house is on fire!" I watched in terror from a neighbor's home as flames engulfed my home, destroying my world.

Time stood still, and I was flooded with grief as I was torn from everything which had nurtured me. I don't remember how I got there, but suddenly I was in Marseille with my parents and my sister. I cried and cried for days. No one talked about the fire. Where was Mémé? My mother tried very hard to make me feel at home, but I just wanted to go to the home where I felt I belonged. She explained that I no longer had a home in Corsica; my home and family were right here in Marseille.

My new home was in the country. There was a vegetable garden, a chicken coop, and a well-kept house with a back-yard. Yet, the house seemed sterile in comparison to the warm atmosphere of Mémé's house; it was also very quiet and even sad. Or maybe the sadness was deep within me.

Everything that enlivened my senses was missing: no cof-fee brewing, no tomatoes drying on the roof, no sea breeze in the evening, no votive candles to make me safe at night and create a world of wonder around me. There was no feeling of connection with the neighbors, no evenings on the balcony, no mornings at the market place, no songs of the fishermen, no statues of Mother Mary on every street corner, no rituals, no "zia" to pray for me. No one knew my name when I went out into the street. There was no place to run to; we were enclosed in a backyard. The little girl who had run like a wild goat was jailed in what seemed to be a foreign, cold universe where no one spoke Corsican like "at home."

Often at night I cried myself to sleep in the bed my sister and I shared. My sister had been the only child for many years; she resented sharing her home with me. I wanted to disappear.

One fine day, Mémé came to visit. She was alive! My hap-piness soared! I had missed her so much!

"Take me home, Mémé," I pleaded. "I don't like it here!"

"I can't, *ma cherie*," Mémé replied. "I'm not allowed to take you, but you'll always be my daughter."

Slowly I closed to the memories of the past as I was asked to, and adjusted to my new life as best I could. I no longer trusted adults, and God had forgotten me. I did not foresee that those memories would surface seventeen years later when I would have my own direct experience of death and the spirit world. I did not foresee that, years later, the shamanic tradition of the island so deeply instilled in me would provide understanding of that experience in the very different culture of a far away country.

From the light
    we have come
And to the light
    we shall return.

Josiane Antonette

CHAPTER TWO

Encounter with Death

I had not expected to encounter my own death so early in life. At twenty-four, the connection with the spirit world I had known as a very young child had long been forgotten. I was a young mother of an active four-year-old son and recently separated from my husband. I had completed nursing school and worked as an assistant in a dental office in Marseille to support my son and myself and maintain our tiny apartment. Like many working mothers, I did not feel particularly fulfilled or happy, but I was so busy working and raising a child there was no time for such thoughts. I considered myself an atheist, and besides, I had no time for spiritual pursuits. I had forgotten God.

My near-death experience shattered my world. It shook me into remembering spirit and other dimensions of life, which I had known as a child but had forgotten so that I could fit into society.

Even now, almost thirty years later as I tell my story, the passion of the moment I encountered death moves me. I remember the ambulance siren shrieking and, as my

Cie des Arts Photoméchaniques, Paris

The house of Napoleon's birth

*Marseille, spring 1949,
after the fire in Corsica.*

CHAPTER TWO

memories become more vivid, I begin to relive my near-death experience:

I feel the jerking of the ambulance as it rushes me through the dark streets of Marseille to the hospital. Twenty-four hours have passed since my underground abortion with a *feuseuse d'anges*, an "angel maker." Abortion is illegal in France now, and many women die because of the unsanitary conditions of the procedure. I am only twenty-four years old, a young nurse. Am I dying?

I feel alone. I want someone to know I'm dying. I try to yell, "I am dying! I'm scared!" No one hears my silent shouts. I cannot speak—I want to scream! I feel so small—lost in an ocean of pain and fear...

Am I outside myself observing? I see my body and its pain. I look at my feet; they are pale and lifeless. My legs cannot move. My face is white and drawn.

I watch as the walls of the ambulance dissolve. I see the lights of the city speed toward me. I can see the stars! What am I doing up so high? Why does everything look so small all of a sudden?

Who is this little girl? She dances in front of me, glances back, and then runs away. Does she want me to follow her? She's so pretty and small. Her legs are dark; so are her arms and face. She has no shoes. I see her run down the street. At the end of the street I can see the sea! I am in Corsica. This little girl is me!

Memories pass before my eyes as in a movie. I'm standing in the middle of the street. It's dark, and I am crying in despair. Our house is on fire! Grandmother refuses to leave. She is trying to save our belongings. My voice echoes in the night, *"Mémé, Mémé, je t'en supplie, descents!"* I try to run to her; people hold me back. No one talks. Some cry. Sadness is everywhere.

My special bedroom! I smell the candles burning; I see the flickering light projecting shadows on the walls and on the paintings against the walls. Grandmother is resting upon her bed; she is sound asleep. Oh, how I love her! And there is my favorite statue: the statue of the child Jesus. It's all made of wax. His eyes are deep, and when I look into them I feel that I'm looking at eternity. Oh, I want to touch it, but I can't. It's supposed to be mine! It was promised to me.

It is the day before Easter. The priest has just come to bless our house as he does every year. We've worked very hard to clean the house. We have repainted the walls. Everything is ready for the blessing. But it's night now, and our house is on fire!

Someone is picking me up, and I am awakened. It's hard to breathe; smoke fills the room. It's so dark, and I'm scared! I cry and kick! The townsmen are here; they've created a chain of bodies from stair to stair all the way from the fourth floor where we live to the street. I feel the strong arms of each man as I am passed down the stairs.

Now I see my best friend moving! Her father died in the fire. I will never see her again! My dog is dead, too, and a cat's newborn kittens. The statue of Jesus has melted.

CHAPTER TWO

Deep sadness fills me, and I start to cry. Suddenly, I'm back in Marseille in the ambulance. I see the ambulance walls, and there is a ceiling. I hear the ambulance driver talking on the radio to the hospital.

The man sitting next to the driver says, "She doesn't look good. You think she's going to make it?"

The driver replies, "She's young. She'll make it."

"Make it," "not make it"—what is happening? Please, someone, tell me!

The ambulance comes to a sudden halt, and we are at the hospital. No one is waiting for us as we enter. The dim light of a long, cold hallway filters across my eyes. We stop at the nurse's desk, and the drivers fill out papers. The nurse glances in my direction; there is no emotion in her eyes. "She is so used to this," I think. She shows the ambulance drivers to the elevator. They load the stretcher, and the elevator rises.

I feel so light. It seems like something is lifting my body from the bed. Tingling fills my lifeless-looking arms. Waves of calm and peace melt into me. The sound of the old elevator fills the silence. I hear it grow louder and louder until it masks my thoughts, pain, fear, and loneliness, and I feel it in my core. I relax. I'm so comfortable! Nothing seems important.

The sound of the elevator door lurching open draws my attention, the stretcher jerks, and intense pain shoots through my abdomen.

"Good luck," the young drivers say as they place the stretcher against a wall near the emergency room. They leave.

Near me a person is lying on a stretcher waiting to be taken care of, I guess. Or is she dead? There is a blood stain on her sheet. Where is her family? Why is she here alone?

Fear, loneliness, and pain grip me.

A woman dressed in white approaches. "The hospital has assigned a very good doctor to your case until your own is available," she says. "You'll like him; you'll see," she adds.

Panic fills my mind. I shiver. "I feel so cold," I whisper.

The woman in white rolls me into the surgery room. The room seems large and white. I hear a group of people murmuring. They approach me. One of them lifts the blanket covering me, glances at my body without making eye contact, and touches my very hard stomach. They leave. I hear their hushed voices once again.

There is a woman in the group. But what am I doing standing next to her? I feel her concern; I know she cares. She leaves the group, and I follow her to the stretcher where my body is resting. I watch as she bends over my body. She caresses my cheek gently. As she touches me, I am within my body again.

"Don't you worry, young lady. I'm going to be the last face you see before you fall asleep, and I'll be the first face you see when you wake up."

"Thank you," I mouth, and reach for her hand. I know that in some way we have touched—soul to soul. Wondrous feelings of love and gratitude settle over me.

* * *

Slowly I try to open my eyes, but it is very difficult. The surgery is over, and I feel paralyzed. Everything is moving in slow motion. Gradually I become somewhat aware of my surroundings: I am resting in bed in a hospital room. Tubes are sticking out of my body; a bag hangs at my side. My family is here! The room is filled with people; they surround my bed. They whisper and talk in low tones.

How difficult it must have been to gather my family; no one has a telephone. But everyone is here: my aunts, uncles, cousins, sister, parents.

I am going to die! They are here because I am going to die!

Memories of Corsica begin to flash through my mind. I remember that when someone was about to die, the relatives and friends all stayed with the dying person until it was over. The room was filled with the same silence, the same sadness. When someone died, the family would send for the wake women, *les pleureuses*—the wailers. For three days during the wake, their loud laments would echo into the night.

I remember the death of my favorite aunt. We all spent three days and two nights around her bed in her own home.

People traveled far by train or boat, and needed to be accommodated for several days. The older women kept food, coffee, and even wine available at all times. Her only daughter had just given birth to a little girl, and the child peacefully lay next to her dead grandmother. It was believed that my aunt could still feel and see her first granddaughter, and no one wanted to deprive her of that joy.

I sense the faint smell of food and again become aware of the hospital room. I know that meals are being prepared by the women and brought to the hospital to be shared by all at my bedside. The customs of generations are being followed.

My family has come to take turns doing what we call *la veille*—a sleepless night shift to make sure that someone is near when I die. In my culture, if I die alone I will not have the proper burial preparations at home; my body will be taken directly to the morgue and cemetery, and that will mean shame for the entire family. Death is a family event—like a christening or wedding—and everyone is expected to participate. It is through such occasions that the family renews its bonds. Death is the most powerful event of all because everyone is reminded of the impermanence of life.

Waves of fatigue wash over me. I try to keep my eyes open, but it is so difficult. I have a deep tiredness, a complete physical exhaustion. I cannot move any part of my body. My death has come, and I am too weak to fight it. I have no choice in the matter.

"Please, don't let me fall asleep again," I whisper to my sister. "Just wake me up if I fall asleep. Just wake me up."

CHAPTER TWO

I view her through a haze. Alice's young face is pale with concern and the many sleepless hours at my bedside. I turn to her for my comfort. I cling to her for life. I know she understands what is happening and has no judgment and shame about my predicament. I feel the soft mound of pillows she jams behind my back so I will be sitting instead of lying down; this way I have a chance to stay awake.

My eyes cannot focus, and my entire body feels weightless.

Someone murmurs, "Look at her eyes and her nose. She's not going to last very long."

Another responds, "But she's so young..."

"Don't say that. I'm here!" I shout in my mind. "I hear you!"

I see family members at the foot of my bed through a haze. Suddenly they disappear. From where they stood I see faces rushing toward me with incredible speed. They race toward my face, expanding then dissolving. Face after face washes over me! I am terrified. I'm drifting. I'm unable to keep my eyes open. Who are these people? Some I recognize as people I've known who have died. Others I do not recognize. "Stay away!"

Where is my family? Now the whole room is filled with spirits! They hover near me and look into my eyes. I try to push them away. I fight them. The experience seems to go on forever. These are spirits who are restless. Their faces are twisted with pain. They seem lost. It's frightening to see them walking back and forth around my bed.

And now—spirits with glowing faces come close to me. They reflect a gentle and powerful light, reminding me of the pictures of beautiful angels that I love so much. I feel nurtured and loved by them, and enveloped by their luminescence. These beings are made of light, and even though their brilliance is intense, I am not blinded. Tremendous compassionate love surrounds me!

Now—I am filled with the essence of love and compassion. This magnetic power is filling every atom of me. I have never before experienced such depth and power of love. I am the power of love! Merging into an intimate dance wherein all boundaries have disappeared, I feel myself one with these beings of compassion.

No words or sounds are being exchanged, and yet communication is happening. A strong presence assures me, "Yes, you are dying to the world of men. But to us you are being born. Do not be afraid. You have always been with us; we have always been with you. We know you. You just fell asleep during your time on Earth and forgot who you are. Now you are remembering."

Revelation fills my awareness—of course, yes! I am of the beings of light and they are of me!

What is this new surge of energy? It begins as a very gentle vibration rising through the length of my body, from my feet to the top of my head, but now my whole self is vibrating. I hear buzzing. It is growing louder, and now the vibration and the buzzing are becoming one.

CHAPTER TWO

I feel such a wonderful release! I'm free! I can't resist this new and wonderful tide of energy sweeping my body upward. Now I'm on the hospital room ceiling gazing down! Everything appears so small: I see my bed; my body looks small and colorless; the people around the bed are tiny. Overwhelming grief and sorrow fill the room, and yet I feel completely disconnected from the scene below me.

I hover nearer and look at the strange form lying on the bed. I feel compassion beyond words. I understand everything, but I have no feeling of attachment to anyone. I look at each person standing at the bedside and feel tremendous love. I want to say to them, "I'm all right. You don't have to worry. I'm all right. Look at me! I'm fine!"

I am love; I am understanding; I am compassion! My presence fills the room. And now I feel my presence in every room in the hospital. Even the tiniest space in the hospital is filled with this presence that is me. I sense myself beyond the hospital, above the city, even encompassing Earth. I am melting into the universe. I am everywhere at once. I see pulsing light everywhere. Such a loving presence envelopes me!

I hear a voice say, "Life is a precious gift: to love, to care, to share."

Questions race through my awareness: Why is there so much pain in the world? Why are humans made of different colors? Why with different creeds? Why with different languages?

A vision appears. I see our world from the vantage point of a star, or another planet. Earth appears as a sphere cut in half. The surface of the planet is flat and colorless. The ground is bare. No living plant grows from the earth. Tree branches are naked. There are no fruits, no flowers, no leaves. The barren hills are obscured behind a grey veil. It is a passionless place where no one rejoices at the sunrise, and no one knows when night comes. Naked phantom-like people stand on what seems to be a stage. All the actors are puppets animated by an invisible force. They move in unison and stop all at once.

On one side of half of the sphere, a sun attempts to shine upon the stage, but no one pays attention or makes a sound. Even the birds in the dead trees are silent and motionless. The other side of the half sphere is in darkness. I watch as the darkness grows with frightening speed and covers the whole planet. No one pays attention. Now the darkness covers the sunlight, and now it covers all the bright planets in the universe.

"This is the world with the absence of light, love, and free will," the voice states. "It is the people's choices that created the world you have just seen."

With these words, the nightmarish world begins to dissolve and is replaced by the other half of the planet—a place of vibrant, breathtaking beauty. I perceive how the Earth, the sun, the moon, the darkness, the light, the planets, and all forms of life—plants, rocks, animals, people—are interconnected: they come from the same source of light. Everything is united by a transparent net, or web, and each thread shines with great radiance. Everything pulses with the same luminosity—a magnificent light of unparalleled brilliance.

CHAPTER TWO

"From the light we have come, and to the light we all shall return, " continues the voice.

I realize now I have been standing in the middle of the two worlds. And with this understanding, an image of the path I have been walking appears. It is narrow and rocky; I have the sensation of losing my balance. I grow afraid of falling into the darkened planet. Free will! With the remembering, I gaze at my invisible feet. The narrow path changes into a wide road. The darkness is replaced by light.

"Never, never forget." I hear the voice say.

I am so overcome with gratitude and overwhelmed by the love that fills me that I cry.

Suddenly, time and space are different again, and I am momentarily aware of my body.

I am aware that the window to the left of my bed is filled with vibrant, powerful light. It seems to be calling me and pulling me toward it like a magnet. I hear the buzzing again, and… Whoosh! I'm zooming through the window! I merge with the light! I am the light, and the light is me.

"From the light we have come, and to the light we shall all return," repeats the voice.

What a joy to bathe in this incredible all-knowing, all-loving…

I can travel through walls, ceilings, and space at amazing speed! I visit my son, Philippe, who is only four. How

Cousin Jean Pierre at age 21

Pepé (on the far left) at the harbor in Ajaccio, Corsica

innocent he is. I see his little body lying on his bed; dark curls frame his face. I want to hold him and let him know I am here, but I can't. I visit my grandmother in Corsica. She is sitting in the kitchen in her favorite chair. There is food on the table, and it is afternoon. I recognize the particular light that bathes her home in the afternoon and the warmth it gives to the room. I hover over her and watch from the ceiling. Will she see me? She does not. I draw closer to touch Grandmother, to make my presence known. Oh, I cannot touch her.

A tremendous power moves me. I am boundless, formless, no longer controlled by my emotions. I am everything. Everything is me!

I'm back in the hospital room. A mist coming from the door facing my bed attracts my attention. In the middle of the vapor is a being with the most heavenly smile. Jean Pierre! It is my cousin, Jean Pierre! I am overwhelmed with joy.

As I gaze at Jean Pierre, the hospital room disappears. We are suspended in midair. There are no windows or doors, no ceiling or ground. A brilliant radiance fills all space. He slowly approaches my bed and bends to kiss me. I feel the moisture of his lips on my face, the weight of his body against mine, the gentle touch of his hands on me.

Jean Pierre is the brother I never had. After a long and painful battle with lung cancer, he died two years ago when he was only twenty-two. I am still grieving his passing. How wonderful to see him again! And what is this? He is wearing his butterscotch jacket. This jacket has been the subject of many discussions. He loves it; I hate it.

"How did you know I was here?"

My question is a thought not yet put into words as Jean Pierre answers, "We know everything about you, and we welcome you."

Such a warm feeling of peace! I am complete—whole! I am free of pain and fear. There is no past or future—everything is! There is no need to speak to be understood or to communicate. I feel serenity beyond anything I have ever known. And joy of joys: I can fly! I swirl easily and with great speed around my cousin in a playful way, expressing the ultimate joy that is me. Everything is the way it should be. Never have I felt so clear, so complete, so loved.

I gaze at myself: I am whole and healed! I can interact and play with Jean Pierre with my natural vigor. Familiar beings of light are here, too. I immerse myself in their loving presence. It's as if they are protecting me and carrying me. We are all interconnected. I relax into the timeless joy. What a glorious feeling! I want to be here forever.

Jean Pierre is gazing at me now as the other beings begin to depart. His dark eyes are filled with great tenderness and purity. He turns to leave with the others, and I plead with him to take me with him. His eyes fill with sadness.

"Not now," he responds. "There is much, much work for you. You have to go back and tell them. Life is a precious gift. Each moment is filled with great opportunities. Don't waste your time on Earth. Spread love and understanding. We will always be with you—guiding you, protecting you, awaiting the time when we will be reunited—when your work on Earth is over."

I watch as Jean Pierre dissolves into the same brilliant light with which he had entered. The light is fading away, too.

The room is empty now. My grief is intense. I start to cry out of desperation and loneliness.

Suddenly, I'm back in the hospital in bed. I am fully aware of my surroundings and my physical state of being. Tubes are implanted in my body. The pain is overwhelming. My sadness is intense. I am so weak I cannot speak. I have lost my voice, and the doctors are alarmed by my tears which are using up the strength I need to recuperate. Crying is all I want to do! My body feels like a suit that is too tight; the room is confining; the smell of sickness surprises my senses; the human condition saddens me.

"Josiane, you're back!" I recognize my sister's voice. I see her careful gaze. "You've been in a coma for three days. We didn't know if you were coming back."

*Learn to get in touch with silence
within yourself
and know that everything in life
has a purpose.
There are no mistakes,
no coincidences.
All events are blessings
given to us to learn from.*

Elizabeth Kubler-Ross

CHAPTER THREE

The Return

I cried for ten days and then gradually regained my voice and began to relate my strange experiences to an audience of family members gathered around my bed.

"So many faces! I saw so many faces racing toward me."

My aunt Angele, sister Alice, and Mother leaned closer to hear my weak voice.

"Some of the people I recognized, like Jean Pierre. But others—I didn't know who they were. I saw a young girl wearing a short white dress. She had big, fluffy, white ribbons in her hair. She came to me several times and seemed to want to talk with me. Her young face was not frightening at all, simply curious, but things were moving so rapidly... I just wanted them all to go away."

Mother gave Aunt Angele a knowing look. "Tell us more about this girl," she said, her voice revealing a sense of wonder. And after I described the girl in detail, she announced, "That was Victoire, my sister. She died just before her first communion when she was only twelve. She was buried in the dress you described. We gave you her name as your middle name in her memory."

"Who else did you see?" Alice asked.

"There was a very young man who came to my attention. He was dressed as an army officer and was quite gentle looking, with dark hair and good posture. He seemed to be very concerned as he approached me. He came back many times, trying to get my attention, I suppose. But I was so frightened that I pushed him away again and again."

"When you were gone," Alice added, "you looked like you were fighting phantoms. We didn't know what was happening to you. We could see nothing, but you were moving your arms and hands in the air like you were trying to push something away."

"I'll bring old family photographs," Aunt Angele offered. "You will see. He was your second cousin on your grandmother's side. He died in the First World War at the age of twenty-five."

"And there was one really scary old woman. She walked back and forth by the foot of my bed. She was small but strong, and she stared at me with such intensity! And her laugh! She sounded like an insane person."

"That was Aunt Gabrielle. She died years ago. When your father and I were first married, we had to live with her a while. We didn't get along at all! What a bitter old woman!" After a long and thoughtful pause, Mother leaned closer and whispered a family secret, "She developed mental disorders shortly before her death."

"But how is this possible? How did the spirits of the departed know to find me? I don't remember ever seeing any pictures of these people." And I continued to describe the many beings who had visited me—people I had known, relatives I had never met, and the beautiful beings of light.

In the days following my coma, sometimes I surprised myself and others by knowing things I should not have known. One day I inquired about Jean Pierre's mother, my aunt, who had visited me in the hospital.

"Why was she so upset and angry when she arrived at the hospital?" I asked. "I saw her enter the room with her head down. She was very withdrawn. She did not even come near to touch me or look in my direction. She simply sat in the corner of the room."

"But how did you know that?" exclaimed my mother. "What you say is true, but she came while you were in a coma!"

"I don't understand how it is possible, but I know. I saw everything that was happening around me. I was aware of many places and realities at the same time. And that dreadful nurse that gave me shots while I was in a coma! She was so harsh and uncaring. I would watch her throughout the hospital as she made her rounds and got closer and closer to me. How I dreaded her approach!"

It was during these days in the hospital that I realized I could now see and sense people's feelings and hear thoughts. I could also see luminosity around people's bodies. Every person was unique, radiating different shades of light and dark, and also colors. These colors changed with people's moods and feelings. I was aware of the gentle light around the nurse who was taking care of me, and the dull grayish light around the sick woman who shared my room.

One time a cousin came to visit. This person had a very happy nature and always smiled. She and I had shared much fun in the past. On the day she came to visit, she was as cheerful as always, but I saw a dark cloud on the left side of her body close to her heart as she entered the room. I did not understand what I saw. Not long after that visit, her husband was killed in a car accident. She became very sad and no longer laughed. I wondered: Did I see her pain before she even experienced it?

Another time a childhood friend came to visit me. There was a gentle luminosity around her—like the one I later saw many times around pregnant women or women who had just given birth. I also felt that she was not alone; a spirit was accompanying her.

"Are you pregnant?" I asked.

"I wish I was!" she replied. "You know how difficult it's been for me."

Eight months later she gave birth to a baby boy. How was it possible for me to see this?

Since childhood I had always been intuitive. But upon my return to Marseille, I unconsciously desensitized to fit into society. I closed my connection with the spirit world. My near-death experience was a catalyst which reminded me of who I was and the special gifts I had been given. Now, what I saw or predicted was being verified in the world, and I realized the importance of trusting my intuition.

Even with my renewed sensitivity, deep inside me I could feel the emptiness left by my experience with the beautiful beings of light and love. I just wanted to go back "home." Being here was a terrible mistake, I felt. I did not belong here.

I spent six weeks in the hospital, and every day was a new challenge as I struggled to adjust to my new awareness and my physical healing. From my hospital bed, I made a silent promise to God: "If I ever walk again, I will serve You for the rest of my life!"

On the day I left, the staff had a good-bye party for me, and I dressed for the first time in over a month. What a shock! My clothes were hanging over my emaciated body, and my legs looked like two sticks swallowed by the vast opening of my boots. I looked like the ghostly people I had seen in concentration camp pictures. My skin was yellow, my eyes sunk in; my hands showed each bone and vein. I was so weak that I almost fainted at the sight.

A nurse came to me and said very gently, "You are young. You'll see. In time you'll be back to your old self."

Someone else said, "While you lay on your bed during your ordeal, I thought you were an old woman. How pretty you are!" Inside I really felt like an old woman.

Each of the hospital staff came to congratulate me for my recovery, and it was then I realized that I was their "miracle." No one had expected me to survive! My doctor explained to me that if my body had not been so strong, I wouldn't have made it. He had also given up on me. He had merely kept me free of pain so nature could take its course.

Alice and my mother were standing next to me. "We have something we must tell you, Josiane," Alice gently said. Her words were hesitant, and I sensed their importance. "You'll be coming home with me."

"What do you mean?" I asked.

Mother and Alice glanced at each other and then looked directly at me.

"We didn't expect you to live, either," Mother explained. "So we gave up your apartment and gave away your belongings."

I left the hospital in a state of shock and moved into my sister's tiny apartment to begin nurturing myself back to health. My losses seemed too great to bear. Depression filled me. Several days later I hemorrhaged and returned to the hospital for more surgery. This time I was fully conscious and not so concerned about death. I knew Jean Pierre and the beings of light were with me; the surgery was successful. Soon I started to move with more ease. Slowly my strength came back. My eyes could focus much better. I regained my voice. Sleep seemed to be the focus of my life as my body healed. My convalescence took a very long time—two years with yet another surgery.

CHAPTER THREE

During this time, I struggled to integrate my new awareness into my life. Sometimes I was depressed, and doubt and judgment about my experiences would dominate. Other times, I could understand my experiences with the afterlife and the messages I had received. Sleep became my escape into the world I missed so much, until I began to accept the fact that I was part of the living and began to focus on my recovery and my responsibility as a mother. I was fragile, but I was part of the living.

Now what I had to do was reconcile and integrate into my life the new awareness I had gained through my experience with death. This was the hardest task I ever challenged myself with, but also the most rewarding. The road to recovery happened to be long and not always straightforward. Since I did not see things the same way—events and people—as before my experience, I was constantly challenged by life.

When I looked at the interactions between people, for example, I was aware that most people avoided being fully present with one another, and this saddened me. The cruelty shown to animals, and anything considered inferior to human life, was heartbreaking. I realized that everything happening around me was part of me since we are all part of one whole. I felt ashamed of being "human" whenever I witnessed people betray their true nature over and over with no awareness of what they were doing.

In a burst of frustration, once I threw a small potted plant against the wall to release my anger. As soon as this act took place, I realized the consequence of my action. I felt terribly ashamed for the harm I had created and for taking away a life. Everyone laughed at my silliness when I started to cry, but I chose then never to inflict this type of violence again, as I knew the preciousness of life. I knew that if it is true that all life is interconnected, then my action was going to ripple throughout all consciousness. I had disturbed the flow of nature. On many occasions I was challenged by life to stand up for what I knew to be true and to stay in the integrity of my awareness.

Once, I witnessed a car accident in which a mother and her young son were killed. Despite the shocking scene, within me I felt calm and assured that everything was fine. Everyone else at the scene was frantic. Some were even hysterical.

As I stood there silently, I was suddenly very remote from the physical world; I heard no sound, felt no one, time stood still for a moment, and I became aware of what appeared as a light smoke coming out of their bodies and slowly dissipating. I was in awe of the gentleness and beauty of the event.

Friends asked me why I had been so quiet and cold. "Weren't you touched by what happened?" they asked.

"Of course," I answered. I did not tell them I had been reminded that life goes on in a new way. I knew the mother and her son understood this now, too. Somehow, I knew that they were at peace.

Sometimes friends and family members were angry with me for not behaving as they felt I should. They were having a difficult time accepting my new way of being. I was set apart from old friends and family, and I felt alienated from the ones I loved.

What seemed so important to most people did not interest me much. Yet, I was alive, and if I was alive I was going to try to live like everyone else. The promise I had made to God when I was in bed—to serve Him if he gave me back my life—did not seem very important. I was struggling to integrate my new awareness and to be in the world. I felt pulled in many directions simultaneously and constantly challenged. All life had become so precious to me that, for a while, I could not eat meat or see blood. It was a constant reminder of our human ignorance. Despite my tremendous desire to belong in the "real" world, I was surrendering to my new awareness and perception of what others could not feel or see.

No matter how painful or pleasant my life events were, an incredible force pushed me onward. Sometimes reluctantly, sometimes with open arms, I was forced to change. It was as if an irresistible current was carrying me from one discovery to another, one experience to the next. I could only surrender.

I came to realize how artificially cramped I was, how I let cultural beliefs and values create my identity and define the world. How had I identified so much with the physical aspect of my existence that I had forgotten who I truly was?

I felt like an early explorer who discovered that the world was not flat, but round. I had ventured into the unknown and returned to tell an absurd tale: there was life after life. My testimony was doubted or smiled at, even by people who believed in God. In desperation, I sought the advice of a wise man who had helped me in my spiritual search.

Mr. Barucca was a simple man. One time his wife was ill, and the medical profession tried everything but his wife remained ill. Since he was a spiritual man, even though he did not belong to a church, he and his wife prayed together and asked for her healing. One night he had a dream in which he was shown a certain bookstore on a specific street and told that he would find a cure for his wife there. He listened to the message, went to the store, found the book, and healed his wife. When people heard of Mr. Barucca's experience, many flocked to his door. I was one of them. My mother had sent my sister and me to him for counseling before, and I thought perhaps he could help me understand my encounter with death.

At our meeting, I shared my near death experience, telling him about Jean Pierre and how sad I was to be sent back to this world. Mr. Barucca had known my cousin very well, as he had helped him and his family during his illness and death.

"Josiane," he said, "you think it was a dream, don't you? This is why you are here." Mr. Barucca looked squarely into my eyes. "Well, it really happened! You ask why your beloved cousin came to you in this way. When you had a glimpse of the afterlife, would you have believed it if it weren't coming from someone you trusted? Someone who you knew had died and was on the other side?"

"I always have to experience something myself to believe it," I answered. "Maybe not. I have been wondering why—after being in the presence of angels, merging with the light, being able to travel at great speed through physical materials like walls and ceilings, being taught the mysteries of life and witnessing the oneness of all things—it was my cousin who came to tell me I couldn't stay on the other side of life."

"God wanted you to know, and wanted greatly for you to remember when you were called back to life so you could share your experience with others. You are blessed beyond words. You will go to distant places and help many people of all races."

Mr. Barucca's words felt solid and clean. But, "How can anyone believe my story when I cannot even grasp the meaning of it all?" I thought, and left his office feeling more puzzled than ever.

You should realize that your soul suffers if you don't listen to its voice.

Resolve to keep a quiet time during your everyday life. Then your soul can speak to you without being drowned by your own busy-ness.

Albert Schweitzer

CHAPTER FOUR

Voices from the Other Side

Everything seemed new to me; I was observing the world with fresh eyes. My parents had recently moved to the United States from France, and they asked me to join them. I followed them to San Francisco with my son, leaving behind what little seemed comfortable and familiar to me. The culture was very different, and I did not speak the language.

I began to create a new life and put my near-death experience behind me. Although I was educated as a nurse, I worked as a maid and developed a rudimentary grasp of English. I was like a child learning how to walk, and talk, and relate to a new environment!

Then I met the man who would be my husband for the next sixteen years, and a son was born to us. My family was complete. We became very involved in the restaurant business and worked extremely hard. We owned everything that money could buy, but inside of me was a longing. I didn't see the beauty I had experienced while on the other side of life reflected anywhere in this world; I longed for it. My saving grace was the love my two sons and I shared and my responsiblities as a mother and a wife.

In our backyard was a small two-room building. One of the rooms was a darkroom; its walls were covered with black paper. I chose this room as my own. I made an altar in the center which was lit only by candles and decorated with votive pictures. When I had time alone during the day, I went there to pray and contemplate. In the darkness and warmth of the room, I felt safe and somehow "more full" than during my busy working hours.

At night in my dreams, I ran from a man who constantly tracked me. Night after night, I heard his footsteps behind me. I could not see him, and I was too terrified to glance in his direction. Surely meeting him would mean my death! Then one night I came face-to-face with him!

Again, in my dream I was running from him. My hard breathing stung my lungs. My heart beat rapidly in my throat as my feet pounded the stone street. I knew the place; it was a familiar street in Corsica, but now it was deserted. Panic filled my head and blurred my eyesight. His footsteps grew louder and louder. He was drawing closer! On and on I ran to the end of the street. The street ended on a cliff overlooking the sea. Should I jump to escape?

I whirled about to face him.

Standing before me was a being of incredible beauty! A magnificent light surrounded him. He radiated such love and warmth.

CHAPTER FOUR

"I have been waiting twelve years for you," the being said. Then his image disappeared, and the dream ended.

After that, the man of incredible beauty came to me in my dreams almost every night for at least a year, and I welcomed him. Of course, I wanted to see him. Oh, what love I felt! His presence amazed me. I looked forward to going to bed at night, meeting him, and receiving the visions and stories he brought me.

Sometimes I did not understand the meaning of his lessons, and sometimes I did. Always, they made me examine my life and consider my actions.

One night, the man of incredible beauty told me a parable. A vision appeared, and the story unfolded as a movie as he began to speak:

> "Once there were three men. The first was a teacher, a man with great confidence in what he had learned. His knowledge was his whole life. In that sense, he was, indeed, a good teacher, but inside of him was an emptiness that he could not identify. Every day he faced the great responsibility of molding the young minds coming to his class, talking about what he had learned and how important education was, and giving the young people lots of homework.
>
> "One day after school when everyone was gone and the classroom was empty, he be-

came aware of an unseen presence. That terrified him. He looked in every corner of the room and every closet, but could find nothing. The presence was so powerful that he panicked, ran from the room, and realized he was alone in the school.

"He then became aware of a great light coming from the end of the hallway. The light was growing, growing, and growing! No matter where he ran, the light was there. He was so afraid! Soon, he could no longer run and cowered against a wall. The light came toward him slowly. When it reached him, his whole body was filled with an energy so great that he could not sustain it, and he died.

"The second man was a preacher. What a good preacher he was! His congregation was composed of wonderful people—all good Christians. They came to church every Sunday where the preacher gave sermons and made sure there were no sinners among his flock. Anything that was not Christian, he said, was to be feared as the work of the devil. He was very satisfied with his life, but inside of him was an emptiness he could not identify.

CHAPTER FOUR

"That winter after a Sunday mass, while he was getting ready to close the church, he became aware of an unseen presence. That terrified him! 'This is the devil—I am sure!' he thought. 'I will fight this darkness with prayers!' But the presence became stronger, stronger, and stronger! 'Oh, God, please, don't let me down,' he pleaded.

"The preacher then perceived a great light coming from under the church door. The light grew bigger and bigger and soon filled the entire church. The preacher started to run from the light. He jumped into the darkness outside of the church and ran into the street of the town. He soon realized the town was empty! He was alone and terrified! No matter where he ran, the light was there! Soon he could no longer run, and he decided to face the light. The light came slowly. When it reached the preacher, his whole body was filled with an energy so great that the man could not sustain it, and he died.

"The third man was homeless. Every day he went along the streets picking up garbage to feed, clothe, and shelter himself. For the people of the town, he was too dirty. They tolerated him, but told their children to stay away from him as he was surely evil. The

teacher was too educated to talk with him. The preacher was too holy to be with him and only prayed for him. So the old man lived his life alone. He was not educated, and he was not religious, but there was no emptiness in him. Every day upon awakening, summer or winter, he gave thanks to the One who created everything for his life, for the food he gathered, and for the shelter nature offered him. He never feared to lose anything, for he owned nothing.

"One day the people of the town became aware of an unseen presence, and everyone grew restless. Soon they saw a brilliant light coming from the south of town where the old man had found shelter. The light grew bigger and bigger. Some of the people ran with fear. Some gathered together and decided to see what the light was. Together they marched toward it. When they arrived, there in the middle of a blinding light was the old man smiling at them. No longer did he appear poor. He looked like a king all dressed in gold and precious stones. He motioned them to come closer and to listen to the story of the three men. As they approached him, their bodies were filled with a light so great they were transformed!"

CHAPTER FOUR

For the longest time I was puzzled by this parable. Then I realized it reflected my own life struggle to make choices between doing what society expected of me or listening to the call of my own spirit. It was a message telling me to examine my own judgments toward myself and the conditioning which dictated who I was and how to be in the world. I began to acknowledge my own limitations, and slowly my life started to improve.

At night I lived in the world of spirit, and during the day I raised two children and helped my husband in our restaurant business. I was living in two very different, disconnected worlds. Slowly I began to notice my spirit world encroaching upon my everyday reality. One morning, hearing a bird singing, I ran to the window to look and to my great surprise I could understand what the little creature was saying! Other times, I became aware of a strong light around trees and plants, and people, too. Later, I would lie down for about an hour every day and ask the man of incredible beauty to come and teach me.

Once, during what I understood later to be a trance, I witnessed an accident in my mind's eye: A young woman was caught in a burning car and was unable to escape; I felt her fear and pain. Later, I heard on the radio that, indeed, a young woman of thirteen had died in a car fire at the time of my experience.

With all the dreams and visions I was receiving, I was concerned. What was happening to me? One night before falling asleep, I asked for an answer, "God, what is going on? Please, give me the key. What am I to do with these dreams?"

That night I dreamed I was in a gallery. Beautiful paintings hung on the walls. The rest of the room was empty except for a large table in the center. Something in the middle of the table caught my eye; it was pulsating with an incredible light. As I approached the table, I saw that the light was coming from a crystal on which my name was written in golden letters. Next to the crystal was a very large key. I picked up the key; a surge of energy shot through my entire body, and I heard a name repeated several times!

When I woke up the next morning, I was puzzled. That day as I traveled with a friend, I related my strange dream to her.

"But the name you heard repeated is the name of my aunt back east!" Frieda exclaimed. "Do you think there is any connection here?"

"I don't know," I answered honestly, and we looked at each other for a quiet moment.

"Let's find out!" my friend shouted excitedly. "We'll go to my house and call her!" Suddenly we were changing directions, driving toward Frieda's home, running to the phone, and listening as we waited for our call to be answered.

"Hi. This is Frieda. May I speak with Aunt..." Her voice stopped as she listened and then politely ended her call.

"Josiane," Frieda said slowly and carefully, fixing her gaze upon me. "My aunt was rushed to the hospital. They don't expect her to live."

CHAPTER FOUR

A few days later we learned that, indeed, Frieda's aunt had died.

Around that time, I was privileged to have an appointment with Hugh Lynn Cayce, the son of the famous "Sleeping Prophet" Edgar Cayce. I was looking for answers and hoped he could give me some clarity. I told Hugh Lynn about my dreams and visions, the thirteen-year-old in the fire, and Frieda's aunt. Hugh Lynn was gentle yet persuasive with me. He talked about "responding to my call," accomplishing the work I came to do the second time around, fulfilling the responsibility that comes with the gift of prophecy, enduring the loneliness I would feel as the people I love the most might be the last to believe in me, and that it seemed I had "been called to work with lost souls to show them the way home." His words confused me, but also challenged me to resolve the dilemma of living in two worlds.

One night in my dreams, I found myself in a place with many books. Across the room from me, a door opened and the man of incredible beauty entered. How happy I was to see him! I could clearly see his radiant face and blue eyes framed by curly blonde hair. I wanted to run to him. He greeted me and motioned for me to be still and listen.

"I have come to say good-bye," he said as he remained standing. "My time with you is over." The door was slightly ajar, and I could see brilliant light behind it.

"No! Oh, no!" I cried out.

Suddenly my attention was drawn to the opposite side of the room. There under a window on a large wooden bench sat a very petite woman wearing the habit of a Catholic nun.

"We won't meet again this way for a long time," the man of incredible beauty added as he gazed at me with compassion.

When the message was delivered, the image faded, and I awoke from my dream. How I grieved! I never saw the man of incredible beauty again.

A few weeks later, I dreamed I heard beautiful voices singing a sweet melody. As I entered a theater, I realized that I was the only person in the room except the choir on the stage. The music was enthralling! I was mesmerized. Such love and warmth filled the entire theater! The entire choir was dressed in white, and an incredible light surrounded the group. I realized they were angels. What I thought to be a melody was actually my name being repeated over and over by their harmonious voices.

One of the angels left the choir and motioned for me to come to the stage. I was drawn to the center and thoroughly bathed in the most peaceful radiance, as they enfolded me in their protective wings. A strong yet gentle energy infused my entire body as the choir continued to sing my name.

Then the choir opened to reveal the center of the stage and vanished. There she was! It was the nun I had seen when the man of incredible beauty said good-bye! The angels had lured me to her; they had tricked me!

She motioned for me to stay, and I stood there. The choir was gone now. The young sister and I stood in the middle of the stage and looked at each other.

"I am Bernadette," she said simply, and the dream ended.

*They know me not, who think
that I am only flesh and blood,
a transient dweller on this
fragile ship earth that gave me birth.
For I am spirit, eternal, indestructible,
not confined by space or by time.
And when my sojourn here is through
I will move on to other mansions, roles,
assignments in our Creator's
house of eternal life.*

J. Sig Paulson

Touching the Face of the Great Mystery

Shortly after meeting Bernadette, my life began to change dramatically. I was being carried by an incredible force that swept away my resistance. A friend invited me to go hear a well-known psychic who was speaking in the area. At the event, the psychic gave me information about myself and my gifts that no one but I knew: I had developed clairvoyance—the ability to perceive things not in sight; I was sometimes able to assist healing, and also, go into the dream world with questions and receive answers. In a very short time I became the psychic's helper, and I did healing and clairvoyant consultations. Soon a church in San Francisco asked me to work with them, and I became an ordained minister. My daily activities were revealing the spirit world I so cherished. Throughout the many changes, I received the guidance and felt the gentle support of Bernadette.

One day I had a surprise. I came upon a copy of the book *Life of Bernadette*, the story of Bernadette Soubirous, a

Viron

Bernadette Soubirous, the seer of Lourdes.

CHAPTER FIVE

fourteen-year-old French peasant girl to whom Blessed Virgin Mary appeared eighteen times in 1858 at the grotto of Massabielle at Lourdes, and who was canonized Saint Bernadette by Pope Pius XI in 1933. When I opened the book, a picture of Bernadette as a young peasant girl caught my eye. It was she! The sister in my dreams was my Bernadette! Somehow, I had never put two and two together.

As I gazed at the picture, once again I felt the loving presence of Bernadette, and I could smell her body—the musky scent I always smelled when she was near.

Suddenly my mind was filled with new awareness. Bernadette was not a "saint" but a beautiful, earthy, passionate woman with great gifts. She had sacrificed her common dreams of all women—dreams of being a lover and a mother—for the good of her family and, eventually, mankind.

From that moment on, I accepted Bernadette, and we became co-workers. Within a year of meeting Bernadette, I created the Bernadette Foundation, a nonprofit interfaith organization, with the hope of inspiring a gentle change in the way we look at death and care for the dying, and the way we look at life and care for the living. The foundation soon became an important Northern California resource for institutions dealing with aging, death, and dying, as well as for individuals interested in self-healing and spiritual development.

Doors continued to open for me. I was asked by a doctor at one of the largest hospitals in Sonoma County to become a chaplain; I was assigned to the intensive care unit, coronary care unit, and children's surgery and medical unit, and I started my work immediately. I soon became a respected hospital chaplain—the first chaplain ordained by a nontraditional church in the history of Sonoma County. That same summer I was asked to handle the pastoral care for the entire county.

Both my sons were in grade school by then, and I was still working with my husband in our French restaurant five evenings a week. The Bernadette Foundation operated out of our home, and I served as a chaplain at the hospital three days a week. My husband and I even raised many of the vegetables for the restaurant in our backyard garden. With all the roles I was filling, in addition to that of raising two sons, sometimes my husband and I were watering the garden at two o'clock in the morning!

My work as a spiritual counselor was my passion! Never once did I refuse an emergency call. I was learning so much so quickly and was so well received that I did not even have to think for answers or be afraid of questions. My work was as natural to me as breathing air. I was in my element! I now had the opportunity to put into practice what I had learned during my close encounter with death.

Once I was called to see a woman who had kidney failure. Her family was trying to prolong her life and had convinced her to go through dialysis treatment against her wishes. The woman was very angry when I met her: She did not want dialysis, yet she was afraid of not undergoing it! I promised her that I would be with her each time as the experience was difficult, and sometimes she had to stay long hours until her blood coagulated.

One time I said, "Let me help, please," and I placed my hand on her arm. A few seconds later when the nurse came to check her, everything was fine.

This went on for a number of sessions and became our secret. We giggled about it and became good friends. Then one day a male nurse—who seemed a little more aware than the others—came to us.

"Wait a minute! What is going on here? Who are you?" he demanded.

I was frozen with fear. We were caught! Did this mean I would not be permitted to assist any more?

But, no! After this incident, when there was difficulty with a patient, this man and other nurses asked me to help. As far as they were concerned, I came to pray with people. No one questioned or challenged me. It was just a fact, and that was that!

At the Bernadette Foundation office, I worked directly with people, conducting consultations and healing. In the hospital setting, I served as a chaplain and ministered to the "needs of the soul," as one doctor put it. He had reprimanded me for remarking on the needs of a patient. "You take care of the soul, Reverend, and I'll take care of the body," he had sarcastically remarked as he brushed my request aside.

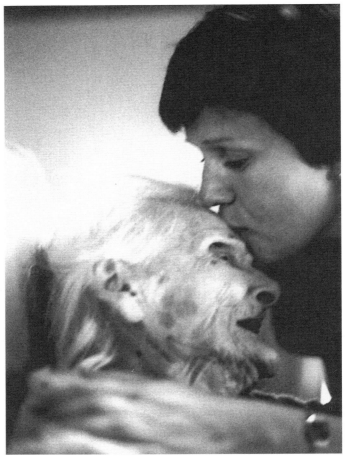

Chaplain Josiane comforting a 100-year-old patient.

CHAPTER FIVE

In the hospital, I became intensely involved with people of all ages going through the transition that we call 'death.' One of my first patients was only twenty-eight when she died of cancer.

When I entered June's room for the first time, she was looking out the window, and I could see only her back. As she turned to greet me I realized how young she was. Her face reflected a pain so immense that I did not know what to say. I stood there speechless. The only thing that came to my mind was: "Please, God, help me! What am I to do?"

For a while we looked at each other, and as I approached her bed she started to cry. I held her in my arms, and she opened her heart to me. We were no longer strangers. She told me of her concern about leaving behind her little girls of four and seven, whom she loved so much.

During the months I shared with her in the hospital or at her home, she experienced many changes of mood and physical ups and downs. Sometimes "I am going to fight this" was the way she greeted me, and we worked together. Other times she did not want to talk with me, and I just stayed in the backyard with the children, learning how important it was to make myself available, but allowing her to have the lead in our relationship and the control which she no longer had in so much of her life. Later she would call me at home to say: "I'm sorry. Please, do not give up on me."

One time June had a dream. In it she was picking fruit with her family at an Indian camp. An old man at a teepee

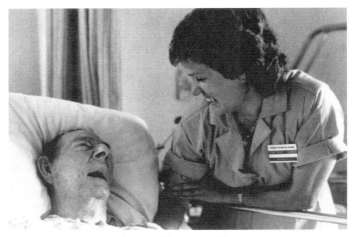

Josiane visiting with some of her patients.

motioned for her to come in. When she turned to tell her family she was going in, she saw them leaving in their family car without her. She ran to tell them to wait, but they only looked at her sadly and waved good-bye. She turned again and entered the teepee.

"What is the meaning of this?" June asked me. We talked about the dream, and she herself concluded that the dream was foretelling her impending death.

June seemed changed after the dream. She started to let her husband spend more time with the girls and was less demanding of his time. She became more silent—as if withdrawing from within. Each time I visited her, I was awed by her strength and ability to make herself as small as possible so her children could have a sense of continuity with their only healthy parent—their father. Sometimes we spent long hours in silence, not needing to explain the inexplicable. Sometimes I knew she felt frightfully alone in her pain, because no matter how much we all loved her, she was the one going through it, and no one could follow her to where she was going.

The day she died, I was called to give her the last rites. She looked beautiful in a bed that now seemed too big for her tiny frame. The room was filled with a soft light— the sort of light you can feel more than see—not a physical light but a transparent haze as if the veil between the two sides of life is being lifted. In her unconscious state, June's face looked radiant. There was no trace of sickness. I could see a vibrant energy expanding and pulsating around her body and encompassing the entire room. When I touched her hand to say good-bye, I knew she was aware of my presence. By allowing me to assist her, June had shared with me one of the most intimate moments of her life: her encounter with the great mystery, the other side of life.

Hugh Lynn Cayce had told me that my love for God, the Creator of all things, would grow stronger through my work. Now I started to understand what he had meant. I could see the Creator in each of my patients and touch the face of the great mystery as I walked with them to the threshold of eternity.

A thirteen-year-old boy dying of leukemia was also a great teacher to me. Despite his parents' knowledge of his impending death, they had taken him to the hospital. I was called to his bed a few days before he died, and in the very short time we spent together he was an inspiration to me.

Peter was a normal boy of his age with the same needs, hopes, and hunger for life, but he also possessed something very special, something only people with long illnesses have in common: a different way of seeing and appreciating things we usually take for granted. The reality of his imminent passing brought many privileges, and he learned very early to challenge everything around him, including his caretakers.

Sometimes when I visited him, if he had a bad day, or had another intrusive medical test, he greeted me with: "What do you want?" or "Do you really enjoy seeing people suffering?"

Once he asked, "Why did my parents take me to the hospital? I was much more comfortable at home!"

CHAPTER FIVE

"They try to do the best they can for you so you can get better," I lied stupidly.

"Who are you trying to fool? Me? Yourself?" he retorted. "Please, Reverend, not you, too. It's enough for me to deal with my parents. I know I am dying. I won't leave this hospital alive. So what's all this fuss about?"

I was caught in my lie. From that moment on we decided to be honest with each other. It was a great relief for both of us. Over and over he tested my ability to be present, and when he was sure of my total attention, he shared his fear of dying and his hope for an afterlife. This boy who had fought disease most of his life talked about his guilt for his anger when he couldn't play like other children, how hard he had been with his parents at times, how he was sad that he would never marry and have children, how he wished he would have had a sibling so his parents would not be too alone when he left.

One time he confided that when very young, he used to play with invisible friends, and that lately they had been around. He had seen them again. He wondered, "Am I going to meet them when I get there?"

"Certainly!" I replied.

Peter made me promise not to tell his parents about our conversations. I asked, "Why?"

"They will be too sad to know I'm looking forward to going, but I've been so tired for so long that I'm looking forward to being free of this sick body. I am worried for my parents;

I don't know how they're going to take this. Would you look after them, Reverend?"

How often I saw this scenario repeated: the dying lying to the living; the living lying to the dying. Everyone afraid of being honest and thereby depriving themselves of truly knowing another human being in the fullness of an experience.

No one has control over life and death and the pain death brings. We only have control over the way we handle both. Peter taught me the importance of honestly expressing feelings with the living and the dying.

When I last saw Peter, God had compassionately taken all the pain away, and he rested motionless in his hospital bed. He was so weak he could hardly talk, but he repeated over and over, "Please, Mom, do not worry for me. I'll be OK. Please…" His desire to protect his parents seemed stronger than his body. There was a glow about him seldom seen around adults facing death. His face, which was slightly turned toward his parents, had an inner smile— not a smile of this world, but an all-knowing smile.

After a while there was breath, another breath, and no breath. He had taken his flight, and I knew his invisible friends were with him then. Later I shared with his parents some of the conversations I had with Peter. Despite their intense grief, they were relieved to know that their son was happy.

I had such compassion for them and understood their pain because I, too, had faced the possible loss of a son. When my youngest son was five months old, he was diagnosed with tuberculosis. Our baby was taken from his father and me for eight long months as he battled death and underwent many painful, intrusive measures to save his life. The torture inflicted upon his frail body was crushingly painful to witness. I felt angry, resentful, and cheated out of my role as a mother. The only thing I knew to do was hold him in my arms and tell him I would never abandon him. We were lucky; our son recovered. My son's illness taught me to take nothing for granted and to savor love in each precious moment.

The anguish of losing a child was painfully reflected in the eyes of Peter's parents, and I gently shared their suffering even as I understood that children are teachers—little angels sent to remind us that the only thing important in life is love given and shared. Only love carries us through life and continues beyond.

This child was a teacher to many of us, especially his family. I knew he had gone back "home." I was also very aware that during his last days in the hospital, he understood what was happening, and it was a natural experience for him. His face reflected divine light.

"Could it be that some of us choose to come for a very short time to finish a certain assignment, and when we are finished we go back 'home' to get our next?" I asked as I went into my dream time.

"At the time of birth," the answer came, "we have already chosen the incarnation which will serve us the most in our growth. It is not the length of one's life that counts;

rather, it is the quality of life we have lived, however short or long, that matters. Sharing love is what matters. And even in the spiritual realm, the departed one continues to exist and protect with a love impossible to describe in words."

Some time later, I would receive a greater understanding of this answer when a friend requested I spend the night in her home shortly after her father's death. She had a great need to talk, and sleep was eluding her.

In the middle of the night, I was awakened by a series of tremors. Immediately I thought of an earthquake, but this was different. My body was filled with a powerful vibrating energy.

I tried to call my friend, but the voice which came out of my mouth was not mine! A masculine voice surprised and scared me.

I pleaded with spirit to assist me. Instantly the vibration stopped and a man appeared, standing at the foot of my bed. He was wearing a dark striped suit, a white shirt, and a tie.

"Please, tell my daughter I'm okay," he requested. "I love her. There is no need to grieve. I'll always be there for her." Then he disappeared as suddenly as he had come.

The next morning I described to my friend what had happened. She was comforted by the message I had received for her. It helped her to know that her father cared, as she had lived away from him and felt guilty about not visiting more often.

CHAPTER FIVE

Experiences similar to this happened to me several times, but I soon decided it was not healthy for me to allow departed spirits to reach their loved ones through me by using my body. After much conscious work on my part, spirits manifested to me, either as bodies of light, or came to me in a dream state to let me know the message they wished to convey to me or to a loved one.

One night, for no apparent reason I awoke, and as I couldn't fall asleep again, I got up for a glass of water. When I reached the living room, I noticed the rocking chair moving. I saw a greenish cloud in the form of a body sitting on it. What was going on? I was startled and afraid, and quickly turned on the light. The chair continued to rock, but I could no longer see the image of a person. Nothing happened, and after a while I returned to bed.

Another night soon after that, I had a similar experience. This time I was upset and loudly commanded, "If you have something to convey, whoever you are, please, come forward! Don't sneak up on me, but come forward and speak!"

The chair stopped rocking. This time I saw the figure of a human being made of light get up from the chair and then dissipate. I was motionless, breathless in the dark. Then, just as I had communicated with the beings of light in my near-death experience, I received a transmission of thought without sound.

"Tomorrow, a woman will come to you. You will know what to show her. Tell her then that I have forgiven her."

*Son Jean Pierre celebrating his first birthday
in the hospital.*

Uncle Paul and Aunt Angèle the day of their wedding.

CHAPTER FIVE

The next morning when I got up, I wondered what this communication meant. Later that day, it came to me suddenly. I was putting material together for the healing circle that would meet in my home that day. For a brief moment everything stood still; there was no noise, and I experienced a very altered state of consciousness. When time resumed, I understood what I was to do.

Two new women participated in the healing circle that day. I approached one and said, "Last night, I was asked to give you this. I don't always know why, but I have learned through the years to trust my guidance anymore."

The woman took the material, looked at it, and began to cry. "This image represents my son and me! How did you know? How did you know that it was meant for me?"

Later, in private, we discussed the message I had received. Her son had died the previous year. Their relationship had been strained. He had reached out from the other side of life to give her the forgiveness she needed to live a full life.

Another time, I was spending a weekend away from home. That morning while I was in the dreamy state between sleep and awakened activity, my uncle Paul, who had died of cancer not long before, came to me. He repeated the name "M" and showed me a gathering of people. I realized the vision had an important message, but I did not know its meaning. I knew I had to look for an answer in the world. On Monday morning, after agonizing over who "M" was, I went to work. Next to the coffee machine I noticed a tiny piece of the newspaper—the size of a classified ad—that someone had cut and left there. Ordinarily I would not have paid attention, but today I read the notice. It was the obituary of my dear friend, Madeliene! She had lost her battle with cancer and had died. I left for the funeral at once and arrived just in time. Her husband was flabbergasted to see me.

"How did you find out?" he asked. "I wanted to let you know, but couldn't locate you!"

My contact with spirits filled my everyday life with wonder, and the hospital setting challenged my new discoveries and abilities. I had a tremendous desire to understand more fully the world beyond, and my work in the hospital was forcing me to look into that world through the pain and fear of human experience.

It was in the hospital that I met a young woman named Linda, who would become one of my many teachers. She had come to the hospital in a coma. Most of the staff treated her as a vegetable—someone whose life functioned only on the physical level.

The first time I met Linda, her tortured body seemed small and helpless. From her throat came what we called the "rattle sound," showing that her lungs were filled with fluid. She seemed desperately lonely. Despite the reluctance of the staff to see me "wasting my time," I decided to develop whatever relationship I could with her, even if my efforts seemed futile to others.

Every day I spent quiet time with her, using my silence to go within and see where she was. Was there a place where I could contact her? I noticed that every time someone approached her bed, her body seemed to avoid contact by trying to change position. I realized that only nurses and doctors were visiting, and only to give treatment or talk aloud about her condition. It was obvious to me that she was more aware than anyone wanted to believe.

I remembered my own experiences of being in a coma in a hospital. A nurse caring for me would give me a shot of morphine every four hours. I was so uncomfortable with her handling of my body that I would get very agitated, and even cry, before she came into the room. No one knew that I could hear her coming from two floors below my room! I could not feel the physical pain of the shots, but I certainly could feel her eagerness to do the job quickly and be finished with me. I felt very vulnerable and scared. Later, to her great surprise, without ever having physically seen her before, I recognized her and even knew her name. My discomfort in her presence became so unbearable that my doctor had to relieve her from my care.

I wanted so much for Linda to know she had nothing to fear, that I was there for her. At first, she refused my physical contact. This went on for at least two months; I would sit there in silence, only touching her face gently when I came in and again when I left.

At last, she slowly opened up to me. When I arrived, the rattle sound stopped, and I could feel a gentle push on my hand when I touched her face. I was overwhelmed with joy and thanked her profusely! It was then that our silent communication started. Her response to my presence was obvious to the entire staff, and I could see the puzzled ways they looked at me when I entered Linda's room.

One day while I was sitting there next to my new friend, she let me know that she wanted to see her mother. She was ready to go home! How was I going to tell the hospital staff that Linda had communicated with me?

At our next patient assessment meeting involving nurses, social workers, doctors, and clergy, I said I had dreamed Linda asked me to bring in her mother. (Her mother had to authorize the hospital not to revive her daughter in case of cardiac arrest.) Everyone at the hospital by then was used to my ability to "see" things unseen, or to know something unknown to others. They listened very carefully. After deliberating, they decided that I should call Linda's mother, who hadn't visited her daughter at the hospital because she couldn't bear to see her suffering so.

I made contact, and arranged to meet with her. We planned to discuss Linda's change of status. Before we had a chance to meet, Linda had a cardiac arrest, and despite the efforts of the staff, they couldn't revive her. I realized what Linda's "going home" meant and was very sad, but I also knew it was her choice. She was only thirty-two years old.

That night I had a dream that I did not remember in the morning but knew was very important. As I was driving to work the next day, I was stuck in stand-still traffic. As I turned my head to my right to see what was happening, I saw a beautiful white car next to me. The driver was a youthful black woman dressed all in white who greeted me with a big smile and a kiss. I recognized Linda instantly and suddenly remembered my dream. Linda was in a meadow filled with wild flowers, and she was dancing, saying, "Thank you! Thank you! I am well. I am free!"

I turned around to take another look at the car, but there was no white car and the traffic was still not moving.

After my experience with Linda, there were many instances when I was called to work with comatose patients, and called by family members to help them contact a departed loved one.

I was confronted over and over by the fact that, as a society, we have so identified the body as the self, we will go to any extreme to postpone the natural flow of life and deny our true nature, our impermanence. The degradation of spirit resulting from the torture inflicted on the body, in an effort to defeat death, was excrutiatingly painful for me to witness.

As I embraced death, I began to understand life. I realized how essential it was to live my life with passion—to fearlessly embrace all my experiences, feeling, expressing, sharing, and accepting my joy *as well as* my pain! Only in this way could I allow myself and others to be all that we are.

In the end, it is the simple things—a kind word, a patient ear, a loving hand—that make all the difference in dying, and in living. I was soon to meet some remarkable people who would remind me of that fact.

For once on the face of the earth
let's not speak in any language
Let's stop for one second
and not move so much.
If for once we could do nothing
perhaps a huge silence
Might interrupt this sadness
of never knowing ourselves.

Pablo Neruda

CHAPTER SIX

Remembering

Mary was a blind Native American woman living on a reservation in California. When I first met her, it was like seeing my own grandmother. Through the Bernadette Foundation, I had created a volunteer program to visit the sick and the dying. After a training period, volunteers could visit patients in hospitals, convalescent homes, and private residences. It was through this program that I met Mary. I thought I was coming to serve her, but surely, she was waiting to teach me!

Mary was dark skinned, and her head was crowned by the most beautiful white hair. She wore—just like Mémé—an ankle-length dress and comfortable shoes too big for her tiny feet. She wanted to feed me right away—the same welcome ritual I had experienced in Corsica. Her home was humble and consisted only of two rooms and a bath. The clean, homey dwelling, as well as the objects hanging on the walls, reflected her connection with Spirit and her pride in her past.

*My first Native American mentor, Mary, from a tribe
in Sonoma County, California.*

CHAPTER SIX

She had been blind since the age of forty and was now in her eightieth year. Through her blindness, she had developed "second sight," and I knew she could see right through me! She challenged me with all sorts of things: cleaning her bathroom, making her bed, or cooking. I knew she was trying to discourage me from visiting, to see if my intentions were good or if I would quit coming. But I could read her, too! I was as stubborn as she was. I accepted the challenge to "show" her. Later we would laugh quite often at our funny "debut."

As time went by, I became very fond of Mary and she of me. We spent many hours talking about our childhoods. She relished telling me over and over about summers when her tribe moved from the hills to the river, how she would swim and play all day until dark, when the adults would tell stories around the fire late into the night.

With her, I learned to cook and eat things I never thought were edible, like acorn mash. I learned about animal spirits and guides, the different gifts each brings to our lives, and how we can learn from their strength, endurance, and commitment to their kind.

One day, she described the death and birth rituals of her tribe.

"When a child is born," Mary told me, "an elder of the tribe, usually a grandmother, whispers the child's spirit name in the baby's ear. No one else hears it. Then, at certain times—like when the child is sick—the spirit name is invoked to help the child."

"So, the child has two names—one for the physical body and another name for the soul?" I asked.

"When the child is coming of age," Mary continued, "the elders see if the child can embody the name. If so, then the spirit name is the only name used. But if, because of personality or behavior, the young one cannot live up to the name, it is not used."

Mary paused, touched the warmth of her tea cup, and turned her face to catch the warm afternoon sun shining through a nearby window before continuing.

"When someone dies, somebody from the tribe comes dressed as that person, wearing the clothing of the deceased. Then each person comes in turn and says what must be said—apologizes, or proclaims love, or whatever must be said."

"That reminds me of the wailers in Corsica," I told her. "For three days, they would wail and receive messages from family members to deliver to the dead, like 'When you see my dead father, tell him that I love him!'"

"Sometimes a wife vents her grief to the person representing her husband, she cries and lets the whole tribe see her anguish. When everyone has said what must be said, the ceremony is over and the clothing of the deceased is burned," Mary concluded, and lapsed into a silent moment of private memories.

Mary told me stories of how her people had lost their traditions and language with the coming of the white men, and how her husband—whom she deeply loved—came to feel so helpless, because of their culture's deterioration, that he started to drink and was eventually killed in a fight with a white man.

My love and respect for her grew as I started to understand that she was teaching me the importance of remembering who I was, honoring and preserving the memories of my ancestors because they made me what I am. With Mary's assistance, I started to get in touch with my roots, and shared with her my own childhood, and how similar mine was to hers despite the differences between our cultures. I told her how Mémé used to pray before she cut a new loaf of bread, and how upset she got if we forgot. How, in the summer, the adults would talk outside until late, telling stories of the past or foretelling a future event as we children played in the streets until we were too tired to play anymore. How the whole family—including aunts, uncles, and cousins—went to the beach to pass the time on a hot summer day, while the men caught fish which we cooked in salt water right on the beach. How the boats were blessed with a prayer before the men went to sea— all the rituals that made our lives complete and filled my heart with so much joy.

One day I wanted to take a picture of Mary, and I had helped her dress for the occasion. She held me very tightly and sweetly.

"You and I are sisters in Spirit, you know," she said. Then she touched my face with her weathered hands, feeling me, and added, "You are beautiful, not only on the outside, but inside, too. You'll live a long life and will help many."

Mary was my introduction to Native American culture. At the time, I didn't realize that I was her apprentice and she my first teacher. After her passing, I never went back to the reservation. I missed her too much and could not bear to see her little home empty. I had felt the tension my visits created among the people of the reservation while she was alive, but she was the elder and they respected her wishes. I knew she would approve of my decision, for we were, after all, "sisters in Spirit."

These days I was even busier than before! I was still helping my husband with the family business and raising two sons, but the Bernadette Foundation was growing, too. I managed the volunteer program, continued service as a chaplain in the hospital, and was still developing my healing abilities. In addition, now I was being asked to appear on television and radio shows to discuss my near-death experience.

In 1983 I was asked by Sonoma State University to be on a panel with the prominent professor and researcher on parapsychology, Dr. Stanley Krippner. After the presentation, he invited me to visit him at the Saybrook Institute in San Francisco. Dr. Krippner was very supportive of my work, and he started to refer clients to my office. I was already very involved with hands-on spiritual healing, but now people started coming from all over the world, with all kinds of afflictions; bringing their children, their pets, or asking me to do "remote healing"—healing with the person not present. The responsibility was great, but my life was filled with great joy.

CHAPTER SIX

Once a man came to see me, complaining of shortness of breath and little energy. He said he had trouble with his lungs despite the fact he didn't smoke and took prescribed medications. He lay down on the massage table, and I prayed to God to send me the energy and clarity I needed to help him. As I scanned his energy with my hands, I felt intense heat coming from his body and became aware of the distinct smell of sickness. As my hands hovered over the area where his energy field was very close to his body, I opened my eyes. I had x-ray vision of his lungs! The left lung looked deflated, as if it was totally devoid of air. I proceeded to fill his lungs with energy, and then told him my vision and advised him to see a doctor immediately. The doctor's examination confirmed that his left lung had collapsed.

Another man had a severe case of shingles. The doctor gave him medications, but they did not seem to help, so his wife came to me and asked if I would do a healing for him. I did, and before I left, I asked that they think of me intensely before retiring that night because I would continue the work in my dream time. That night they went to bed and were awakened in the middle of the night by what appeared to be a bright light coming from their window. The old man got up to see what was going on outside, but as he saw nothing he went back to bed. The next morning he slept longer than usual and announced upon waking, "I slept like a baby last night." To the great surprise of the man and his wife, the shingles were gone!

In my healing work, I realized that people do not make themselves sick, but their emptiness, distress, and pain make them vulnerable to illness and accidents. I was very aware that healing always comes from a higher source, and as a healer I was simply working in cooperation with that source and the person receiving the healing.

I had to redefine the meaning of 'healing,' and compassionately support individuals to discover their wholeness through their circumstances. Sometimes I was approached by people who were very attached to being physically well again; I felt their disappointment and pain in the core of my being when death was the outcome. For some, discovering peace within themselves and the meaning of their unique experience promoted healing of the body. For others, healing meant their spirit no longer required their body.

David was a volunteer for the Bernadette Foundation who had been visiting the sick, aged, and dying for more than a year when he discovered he had contacted the AIDS virus. When he came to my office with the news, he announced his plan to take his life to protect his family. He was in a state of shock, and I let him express everything he felt. I knew my role was to help him see how he could turn his predicament into a more positive experience.

Over the next half year, I felt David's struggle. His parents denied he was gay and did not know he had AIDS. He would rather commit suicide than see their shame and feel his guilt. I was faced with a hard dilemna, and had to shoose between my responsibility as a friend and my responsibility as a counselor. Eventually, I contacted his sister, a good friend of mine with whom David was very close and told her of his threatened suicide. David was furious! But as he, his sister, and I worked together, David decided to confront and heal his issues of shame and guilt. He realized what a teacher he could be to his family. As he gradually accepted himself, slowly his family grew to accept who he was and the plight he was living. It wasn't easy for anyone, but eventually his parents came to be the caring and accepting people of whom he had previously only dreamed. He lived the remainder of his life surrounded by love.

After David's death, The Bernadette Foundation received a generous contribution from his family to help facilitate its work. His illness and death had brought his whole family the gifts of closeness, understanding, and love.

In the course of my work, I discovered an important common element: the willingness of the person seeking healing to believe in—and trust—the process. I learned that when you doubt or question the process itself, you cut yourself off from the source and no healing is possible.

A woman who had injured her left leg skiing came to see me. As I worked on her left knee, I received a clear picture of her right knee filled with water, the skin shiny and stretched. Her right knee felt hot as I scanned its energy with my hands. I shared this information with her.

"I didn't hurt that knee!" she sarcastically remarked. "It's the other leg that was hurt."

"I'm sorry; that's the only information I received," I told her. After a few more remarks, we discontinued the healing.

We could no longer continue because she was not receptive.

The next day I received a phone call from the woman, who was now in the hospital. During the night her right knee had started to hurt very badly. In the morning she could not walk as her knee was filled with water.

"Did you create that in my knee?" she asked accusingly. "Or did you really see it before it happened?"

One day a man called my office for his wife. She had cancer of the throat, he explained, and wanted to speak with me about a healing. When she took the phone, her voice was so low and her words came so slowly, I could hardly comprehend what she was saying. I told her to lay on her couch and relax as I was going to do a "remote healing." We made an appointment for the following week.

Two days later, a person came to my office without an appointment and demanded to see me. The woman talked with a very clear loud voice and said, "Josiane, I bet you do not know who I am."

I surely did not!

"You see," she said, holding out her hand, "this ring I am wearing on my finger was bought for me today by my husband. Usually a man buys a ring so his wife will shut up. This ring was given to me because I am talking! I am the woman who had an appointment with you next week, but I could not wait to tell you how happy you have made me!"

CHAPTER SIX

It was the first time in months she could talk and be understood, and the first time since her disease began that she felt well.

One evening, I lay upon the couch feeling exhausted and frustrated. By now I was working full-time with the Bernadette Foundation and as a chaplain in hospitals. My husband and I had argued, and he had accused me of trying to be a saint! The house was quiet, and everyone had gone to bed. I asked Bernadette to please help me resolve the dilemma of living in two worlds. Suddenly, a musky scent mixed with the strong smell of flowers filled the room. I looked up and gasped in disbelief. There standing before me was Bernadette. She was as physical as any of the patients I had seen that day. Old prayers I thought I had long ago forgotten rushed into my mind like a flash flood, and I even made the sign of the cross. I was afraid! Although Bernadette had been my teacher for some time, she had appeared to me only in dreams, not in a physical form. My heart raced!

Bernadette smiled tenderly at me as my body trembled.

"Heaven is not something you deserve," she said. "Heaven is on earth. You create your heaven right here, right now."

I was so scared, I covered my head with a blanket!

"I, too, once believed that heaven is only in the afterlife," Bernadette continued, "but now I know heaven can be created right here, right now." With that, she disappeared.

The scent of flowers lingered in the house, and the next

day everyone wondered where that strange smell had come from.

"I don't know," I lied to them. I was too afraid to tell. After that, Bernadette continued to work with me, but she never manifested as a physical body before me again. I felt blessed beyond words that she had appeared to me, but I was not sure what she was telling me. It took a long time for me to understand her message. At that time, I was struggling to balance my relationship with my husband and family with the spiritual work I had been called to do.

Soon, I was invited to talk about my near-death experience with a well-known chiropractor in the area. Through him I learned about his mentor, Evelyn Eaton, a naturalized American woman of Swiss descent, who had studied in France and, later, was called to live with the Native Americans. She had learned with the Paiute Indians in California and became a pipe carrier at a time when it was unheard of for non-natives to achieve such an honor.

The chiropractor had been in an accident which had nearly cost him his arm. Evelyn Eaton had sweated and prayed for him in her lodge and helped him recover the use of his arm, which was now fully healed. I was enthralled by the story he told of his total recovery and the spiritual lessons he had learned, but it had no immediate impact upon my life. At least, I was not able to foresee that it would.

A few months later, I was awakened in the middle of the night by a tremendously strong pressure on my chest and felt very short of breath. I tried to get up, but couldn't walk. My body began to shake with panic. I tried to call for help, but could not! Then I became aware of a presence in the room.

"My name is Evelyn," it said, "and I came to let you know you have to take over the work. You have been called, but you have not answered!"

Then the presence dissipated, and my body felt normal again. "Called to take over the work, but did not answer?" I was puzzled. Surely this was simply a bad dream.

The next day I had an appointment with the chiropractor. I shared my dream with him.

"But," he paused and thought, "Evelyn Eaton passed away last night!"

The word that I was taking over Evelyn Eaton's work spread like wildfire. Letters poured in, and people arrived at the foundation wanting me to help them in Evelyn's manner. Although I worked with the living, dying, and the dead, bridging the different dimensions as had Evelyn, at that time I was not a pipe carrier and I did not use Native American ceremonies. The only things I could say were: "No, you are mistaken. I am not the one. I am French. I'm not a native of this land. I have an accent! Can't you see it's wrong?" From deep within my soul, I knew it was not the time for me.

A picture of Evelyn in ceremonial regalia holding a great eagle feather arrived in the mail one day. A short note was written on it: "This is the last picture we have of

Evelyn Eaton in ceremonial regalia.

CHAPTER SIX

Evelyn. We know she would want you to have it." There were no signature and no return address, which I thought was odd.

"Evelyn, why is this happening?" I asked over and over.

The reply was always the same: "It's time for you to take over the work!"

I rebelled as I always do when something tries to force me to change or see things in a new way. The more people came, the more I shied away from their demands. My life was just fine the way it was! In fact, I thought it was better than fine. Everything was going along smoothly; at least I thought so. Was I in for a shock!

My husband left me.

"You don't even belong to me in your dreams," he stated flatly. "Your work is no longer compatible with mine."

In fact, our work wasn't compatible. We had sold the first restaurant, and he was working full-time, without my help, remodeling the second. The Bernadette Foundation had become my full-time job, and our family had changed. Our oldest son was twenty, married, and on his own.

My husband left to be with a woman more suitable for him, took our youngest son, who was still a minor living at home, and moved out of state. I was devastated. My grief was immense for the loss of my family. I felt responsible for the breakup. Overnight I had lost what I loved the most: my son. I did not take legal action for custody because I didn't want my son to go through the agony of choosing one parent over the other; I knew he loved us both. Surely I had been a bad wife and mother for pursuing what I believed was my calling; I deserved the punishment of losing my family. I accepted my fate.

My need for healing was so great that I was forced to explore different ways of dealing with my pain. I became a student of a Kahuna teacher and studied the mind, exploring how my conditioning and beliefs were limiting me. The Huna teaching—the ancient Hawaiian science of the mind—gave me a solid foundation upon which to rebuild my life. Then one day a friend invited me to go to a Native American sweat lodge ceremony held by a Karuk elder named Red Hawk.

When I arrived at the ceremony site, people were standing next to a hot fire singing with the beat of a drum played by a dark-skinned man. Something deep within me felt excited! Soon Red Hawk announced with a deep voice that it was time to start the ceremony. He asked everyone attending for the first time to raise their hands.

Timidly I raised my hand. Red Hawk looked at me, and all of a sudden I felt very small. I could see he knew how I felt. His eyes reflected amusement, but also a paternal strength.

"Welcome," he said, and then summoned me to pray and sweat for what I needed.

The round lodge was about five feet high in its center, the door was about three feet high, and the outside of the lodge was covered with blankets. People began to crawl into the lodge.

When my turn came and Red Hawk motioned me to enter, I wanted to run away! I was terribly self-conscious, and fear grabbed my entire body as I entered the dark, crowded space.

I must have looked like a novice because the woman sitting between my friend and me whispered in a low voice, "If you get scared, hold my hand," which only added to my discomfort.

The leader then said, "If anyone wants to leave at any moment, please, do not hesitate to ask. But I suggest that you try to stay as long as you can, not for me, but for yourself. The less you listen to your mind and your fears, the more you will experience the Divine."

Soon the hot rocks were brought in, and the door was closed. Everything went dark except for the red, glowing light of the rocks. The medicine man put some sacred herbs on the stones and called on the six directions and the Great Spirit to assist in the lodge. Then water was tossed on the stones, and a suffocating hot steam filled the lodge as he sang in his native language. Then—more water, more steam, more chants, more heat!

I felt claustrophobic and thirsty. Sweat poured out from the top of my head to the tips of my toes. Every pore of my body was forced to relinquish any water it held. I was certain I was going to die as I felt myself leaving my body. Part of me wanted to leave the lodge, but I was too proud to ask for the door to be opened. Part of me wanted to stay and break through the resistance.

As I sat in the hot, steamy darkness, slowly I opened. I did not die. I felt more alive than ever! I touched my pain, and I wept openly. The medicine man had called the lodge the "womb of the mother." I remembered my need to be in silence after my near-death experience, and I recalled the dark room in which I prayed and again touched that healing silence. Yes, the womb! I could heal my pain in the womb of the great mother.

When the door finally opened after the sweat, my face was red and swollen, but I felt purged. Red Hawk ushered us out of the lodge to an ice-cold creek close by. I hesitated to enter the stream, but Red Hawk motioned me to come. He held my head under the water for a time that seemed too long. When I emerged, the whole group was standing around me joyfully chanting to congratulate me on my accomplishment.

Slowly I began to understand why I had been brought to Mary, and Red Hawk, and others who would introduce me to what I called "earth spirituality." I considered what Bernadette had shown and told me, and what she had said about heaven on earth. I remembered that each time Bernadette came to me, I could smell her body, and I realized that she had come to teach me the difference between what we think of as "holy," and what is really holy—being whole. Her presence said to me: I have a body; we have bodies; we can fly with angels and live on earth, too. Embrace everything—all parts of yourself—live as spirit and live on earth, too!

CHAPTER SIX

With all the work I had done with death and dying, and my search for how to live fully, I had been focused on spirit and the world beyond. It was time now for me to live my life as a soul and a physical being bridging heaven and earth.

The spark of God, the Soul is in everything
The Universe is a whole in which no one is
alone
Everything alive is a spirit
All flesh is a shroud
And to see the soul
We just have to lift up the shroud

Victor Hugo

Heaven and Earth

Even my dream life was beginning to reflect my new earthiness. My new teachers were worldly creatures as well as celestial beings of light. Birds flew with angels! My angelic teachers had guided me in the celestial world; now my earthly teachers were guiding me into both the terrestial world and the underworld.

One night I awoke with a start. I was between dimensions. I could see the bedroom clearly, and the green light of the clock face told me it was past midnight. I had felt a tremor. The room was still, but my body was trembling.

"What now?" I thought, and tried to reach for the light switch. I had experienced so many unprecedented occurrences in my lifetime that nothing made me too excited any longer.

I couldn't move.

Josiane in ceremonial dress.

CHAPTER SEVEN

I tried again to no avail. My body seemed hypnotized or held prone by some invisible force. A gentle, glowing light surrounded the bed.

Then I saw it.

A huge bird-like creature with outspread wings hovered above me near the ceiling. Its eyes were deep and dark and held me immobile. As it held me transfixed in its gaze, suddenly I was transported.

I found myself standing on a kind of belt that moved me slowly into an unknown area. On each side, I could see people looking in my direction. Some I recognized. I saw my dead friends: Danielle, Michael, Aileen, and David; and my dead pets, Pinpin the cat and Prinz the dog. The outpouring of love from their smiling faces was overwhelming! As I approached, I saw people I had helped through their transitions into death. I recognized some of the hospital patients whom I had loved so much: Linda, Peter, and June. As I passed, each one of them touched me as if in a ritual ceremony. I was so happy to see them all!

Then the belt stopped. I stood in front of a door.

"Come in!" said a voice. I instantly recognized Evelyn's voice—the strong voice that so often asked things of me that I could not comprehend or for which I was not prepared.

The belt moved once again, and I was transported through the door to the middle of a room and onto a rotating platform. I stood alone in the center. As I gazed outward,

I saw my living relatives, friends, and children surrounding the platform. I was happy to see some of them, not happy to see others.

"You have to make peace with each part of yourself to be whole," Evelyn explained. "Therefore, you must make peace with those you have difficulty loving."

Around and around the table-like platform turned, continuing until I saw the glorious light of the Divine in each person and felt unconditional love for them. I had thought unconditional love meant that I must accept all their behaviors. I realized now that in everyone is a part which is always striving for perfection. Unconditional love means honoring that common thread.

"Now you'll never be alone again, for you have seen with the eyes of your soul," she said.

"I have been so blind! How could I feel unconditional love for anyone else, when I couldn't feel that love for myself?" I replied thankfully.

When peace and good will had been established with all my relations and within myself, the table abruptly stopped turning, and I was guided through a door to a pool of milky water where a man and an old woman dressed in white gowns awaited me.

"We bless you for the work you have done with the living, suffering, and the dying," they told me. "However, there is a test you must pass before you may continue your work on Earth."

CHAPTER SEVEN

I stood before them and listened intently.

"You must go through this pool," the two continued. "If you trust, you will go to the other side and live. If you do not, you will die."

My heartbeat raced and shook my chest. My breathing became shallow and quick.

"But...I'm terrified of water!" I retorted.

The man and the old woman simply gazed at me in silence.

Now I realized that, no matter what, I would soon be dead! Terror filled my body. I took a last look around and plunged into the pool.

Milky water entered my ears, eyes and throat. I struggled and held my breath to survive, longer and longer. Surely my chest was collapsing! I could no longer hold my breath. Terror seized my throat as I gasped for air and breathed in the water.

To my surprise, I could breathe under water!

Soon, I was breathing in the water, and the water appeared clear. A gentle hand then reached to me and led me from the pool. I was carried onto a table covered with glowing white linen.

I was alive! I had passed the test.

A gentle hand stroked me. With every touch, light shot from my body. I cried profusely with the joy of accomplishment, and the emotion of seeing others who had failed their tests laid out upon tables around me.

I gazed upward and met the piercing eyes of the bird-like creature hovering above me. Suddenly, I was aware of my bedroom, and I watched as the great winged-creature stretching across the ceiling slowly melted away, and I was able to move again. I glanced at the clock; seven hours had passed.

This was my first conscious experience of the underworld. I did not understand the ramifications of the entire adventure, but I easily saw how, making peace with all my relations in the physical or spirit world, had brought me closer to creating the heaven on earth about which Bernadette had counseled. I realized later that this experience was an initiation, strengthening me for my travels to and from the underworld during my work with lost souls, those trapped between the worlds as a result of their addictions to earthly pleasures or by a sudden death by accident or suicide.

Ever since my first sweat lodge with Red Hawk, I had become more and more aware of my place on Earth and my life as a physical being. Now, I was beginning to understand what it was to be whole, and what Bernadette had meant when she said "we are the keepers of earth, and we have the power to create heaven right here, right now." My awareness of my connection with the universe and all living creatures had expanded to include earth itself and, therefore, more of myself.

CHAPTER SEVEN

At the time, I was very busy with the Bernadette Foundation, working in convalescent homes and developing a special program about understanding the fears and needs of the aging and the dying. I was also teaching a program on death, dying, and healing in several universities. As a respite from my busy schedule, I began to spend more time outdoors. I felt a great hunger for nature, a necessity for me that urban life simply could not provide.

I was now frequently traveling to the small town of Mount Shasta in northern California to participate in the native sweat lodge. In the lodge, I knew myself as a physical being; I sweated, sat on the ground, got dirty, really felt my body and my emotions. But something else important was happening on these trips, too: I was developing a relationship with nature! Most of the first forty years of my life had been lived in urban areas; I had never really explored nature. The lodge sat in a place of impeccable natural grandeur!

The little town of Mount Shasta sits at the foot of the volcanic Mt. Shasta which towers above it at fourteen-thousand feet. The cap of the mountain glistens with glaciers and the clarity of pure mountain air. Transparent water springs up through bubbling earth and ripples past thick green moss, through meadows of springtime pink heather, brilliant red paintbrush, clear-yellow monkey flowers, and a dazzling spectacle of colors, textures, and scents. Ancient red fir trees majestically stand watch over crystalline snow fields, the playgrounds of sweet singing birds, liquid-eyed deer, and shy black bear. Everywhere, life abounds!

The first time I saw Mt. Shasta, I was traveling with my family. I saw the mountain from a distance, and I was awe-struck. I even wrote a poem and dedicated it to the great mountain. In the poem, I described a "carpet of flowers rolling down to infinity" and "a clear spring coming right from the earth" surrounded by towering cliffs of breathtaking beauty. A year later, I had the opportunity to camp on Mt. Shasta and discovered Panther Meadow. The meadow looked exactly like what I had written in my poem. I was overwhelmed! A beautiful spring bubbled up from the earth itself at the head of the meadow. I put my hands in the water over and over to awaken from what seemed to be a dream, and to feel the reality of the place. I was moved to tears with the awareness that I finally had come "home" and a vague remembrance of something that had happened long ago. Later that same year, I went to Lourdes to visit the Spring of Massabielle in the south of France where Bernadette had seen her first vision. The spring at Lourdes, just as the one on Mt. Shasta, bubbled directly from the earth.

When I was in nature, I felt alive and whole. When I returned to my urban home, I felt the tragedy of urban life. The earth was suffocated by asphalt. Polluted air clouded the sky. Tainted water was expected to sustain life. How hard it was for my soul to soar in such an environment, to find the substance to sustain its life!

I was alone then; my parents and sister had moved back to the old country. My younger son was still with his father and visited periodically. My older son had just made me a grandmother for the first time. I was free of family obligation and able to travel back and forth between the

CHAPTER SEVEN

city and the splendid alpine nature of Mt. Shasta. Eventually, I bought a modest home at the foot of my beloved mountain, completed my work as a chaplain, and developed some new programs for the Bernadette Foundation that expanded its scope of service and allowed me to work in both natural and urban environments. When I moved to the country, I discovered a deeper sense of myself during the many hours I spent in nature's solitude. I took the time to examine my own life and found dark places I was reluctant to see.

One evening I was informed that a close friend, Richard, had committed suicide. Only three weeks earlier, my childhood friend Danielle had also ended her own life. The deaths of my friends forced me to confront the darkest recesses of my mind and heal myself. Layer after layer, to my amazement, my repressed feelings were revealed and released.

Through my grief I was led to explore difficult questions: "How much pain can a human being sustain before taking his or her life?" "What brings an intelligent, sensitive person to such a dark place?" These questions I still cannot answer. I realized I must walk in someone's shoes before understanding what brings him or her to suicide.

My friends Richard and Danielle contacted me many times from the other side. The first time Richard came he said, "Josiane, you told me how beautiful it was when you died. It's dark here, and I feel lost." I felt his fear, disappointment, and struggle. Gently, I directed him to look for the light. Both Richard and Danielle came to me many times before they finally found their way home.

My grief was intense, and my only solace was earth. I had to feel my connection with everything. The vastness of the landscape, the towering mountains, the running brooks, the endless sky singing to me of the splendor of Great Mystery. I felt Great Mystery within me and discovered that I was renewed. I made a new commitment to life. Chopping wood, shoveling snow, and building fires to heat my home empowered me.

One day, a person came from the city to seek my guidance for his spiritual development. It seemed to me that this person, like many of us, was looking for his spirituality in all the wrong places. I guided him to a place on Mt. Shasta where we silently stood at six thousand feet, looking down into the valley. Stretching before us was a panorama of three mountain ranges. The day was stormy, and gigantic clouds drifted low in the sky. Rays of sunlight shot in angled profusion around the massive clouds, and poured huge shafts of golden light upon the little town in a spectacular display of power and beauty.

I turned to my companion and said, "You see? This is God!"

He stood in silence for a long time, looking at the scene. Then he turned to me and with great reverence responded, "You are lucky. I see only clouds."

He reminded me of myself long ago, before my solitude in nature and my experiences with the sweat lodge. "How sad," I thought, "he is blind."

I, too, had been blind until I took the time to slow down, become still, and see with the eyes of my soul. But I saw so much when my view of the world shifted and I began to consciously savor every moment. I had to feel earth under my feet to realize how alive it is, and to surrender to my need for nurturing to understand the importance of earth for my survival and the survival of all. As I took in the life-giving vitality of the planet, I was of Earth; I felt connected to my own body again. As I recognized the elements which constitute Earth's body, I understood my own body and its seasons. Without respect and honor for Earth, a part of me was more dead than when death had come to me.

For seven years I lived in Mt. Shasta and learned the Native way as a helper of a Native American spiritual leader, Walking Eagle, of the Karuk tribe. I helped build and care for the sweat lodges and assisted in ceremonies. We also taught a few workshops together, including one in France.

Before leaving for France, he honored me with a naming ceremony to publicly express the spirit within me. My name, Cedar Woman, would bridge my spirit self with my physical self, and I would use it only in a sacred way when I led ceremonies or addressed the Great Spirit. I didn't realize it at the time, but the naming ceremony would open me for two shamanic experiences in France.

The first day abroad, Walking Eagle and I decided to stretch our legs by taking a walk in the country. The trip had been long, and I hadn't slept. We walked for at least an hour before we realized we were lost. I was exhausted; I couldn't take one more step. Instantly, a hawk appeared in the middle of the road.

*Walking Eagle and Josiane at a conference on
world religions in France.*

CHAPTER SEVEN

"Stop walking!" I whispered to Walking Eagle. "That hawk is going to fly away if you don't stop!"

"What hawk?" he replied, as I saw the hawk gazing right through me, and looked up at a buffalo skull hanging in a tree above.

He slowly approached and placed his hands on my shoulders. "It's OK," he reassured me. "You're having a shamanic experience. Don't be afraid."

Suddenly everything disappeared, and I started to cry. My heart beat wildly. "I must be very tired. I'm hallucinating!" I shivered.

"Stop your French mind right now," he scolded. "This was a shamanic experience. I won't have your mind trying to explain what can't be explained."

"But, hawks and buffalo skulls... This is for you, not me. I talk with angels."

"There's no difference between angels and hawks," he replied. "They are both messengers from the Great Spirit."

The next night I went to bed early and awoke about three o'clock in the morning and began to read. After a while, I paused and looked up at the ceiling. A white feather floated down slowly toward me, touched my hand, and slipped through my fingers, landing on the book. I glanced in amazement at the words where the feather rested. "...for the aboriginal, birds—especially the hawk and eagle—are what angels are for us, messengers of God." I knew I was in touch with the Great Spirit, and the message was clear.

The sweat lodge in Mt. Shasta, California.

CHAPTER SEVEN

"I told you they were the same," my mentor retorted the next morning when I told him about my experience. "You are so French, Josiane. You have to let go of your mind and accept."

"And you are so Indian, my friend," I joked. Later, we concluded that in a past life he had surely been a French man—as reading and pronouncing French were quite easy for him; and I—with my shamanic experiences and interest in native ways—had certainly been a Native American.

This trip to France was the first time in thirty years that I connected with the French spiritual community. I was reminded of the tremendous changes in me since I had first left my country. I had left as 'Josiane' and returned as 'Cedar Woman'.

Upon our return to the United States, I had the great honor to ordain Walking Eagle a Minister of the Bernadette Foundation.

One beautiful Mt. Shasta spring, I was called to create a sweat lodge on my property near my home. Many people in need of healing were looking for a more gentle way of experiencing sweat lodges than those led by men. I had recently married and felt very supported, grounded, and ready to expand my work. I wanted to share my blessings and help people who came to me, saying they felt empty, had no purpose in life, did not experience spirit, and had lost their connection with their soul. I knew that the lodge served as a great womb of Mother Earth, and those within its shelter found nurturing, healing, and the touch of Great Spirit.

The little town of Mt. Shasta was still asleep as friends gathered to help build my first lodge. Some had come from the nearby mountains, and others had driven all the way from cities. Some were Native Americans, others were not, but all were lovers of the Earth. The air was crisp, and we could feel the early morning chill upon our bodies as the rising sun covered the mountain's slopes with a purple blanket and painted the sky in a rainbow of colors.

Friends had brought lava rocks, wood for the fire, hay for the floor, and plenty of food to be shared after the ceremony. I had risen early that morning and brewed strong French coffee for everyone. Earlier in the summer, I had gathered wild sage in a sacred place in the mountain wilderness and tied the sacred herb into small bundles for the lodge ceremony. Cedar had been harvested and crushed into a fragrant powder. To honor my ancestors, I also brought two very sacred herbs used for healing by the women in the south of France: rosemary, "les mains de dieu"—the hands of God; and lavender, the purifier.

What a joyous moment for all of us as we offered tobacco to Great Spirit and Mother Earth at the nearby Sacramento River where we carefully selected willow branches for the frame of the lodge! By the time we arrived back at the lodge site, the sun was already high overhead. Each person was then smudged for purification as the fragrant smoke from the burning sage was fanned around each body; the men dug the fire pits inside and outside the lodge, and the women gathered materials for the lodge frame. Then, holes for the lodge poles were dug, tobacco blessed each hole, and the willow branches were planted deep in the ground. When the frame was complete, blankets covered the lodge and fresh, golden hay topped with cedar covered the floor.

The completed lodge commanded the site. Red, yellow, black and white ribbons tied to four poles marking the directions flowed in the breeze against a brilliant blue sky. The door opened to the east, facing the powerful sight of the mountain. To the south under a cherry tree, a graceful statue of Mother Mary stood with her arms outstretched in a gesture of acceptance and welcome.

"What is she doing here?" questioned one of my friends.

"What do you mean?" I asked.

"Mary does not belong here!" Jim announced. "This is not traditional!"

"Do I look or sound 'traditional' to you?" I laughed, stroking my light hair and striking a pose to accentuate my petite female body.

"Even if you aren't traditional, you're supposed to do things in a traditional way," another informed me.

I was stunned. To me, the lodge was a prayer house. Similar lodges had been used since antiquity in many cultures. I had created this lodge to help those searching to fill their emptiness with spirituality and healing realize that spirituality is not simply an experience or a specific form; it is what we are. Surely this purpose was at the heart of all religions and spiritual practices. I had built a lodge surrounded by the symbols of all the spiritual traditions— Mother Mary, Buddha, and many others. Mary was part of my heritage and to me represented the mother of all, just as White Buffalo Woman did in the Native American tradition.

"When we sit down together in this lodge to commune with Great Spirit," I explained, "it doesn't matter what religions we each follow, or what cultures we are from. This is about living life right here and now, grounded on our planet where we are, as we are. We each may have different tools, different ways, but there is a part of us that is the same. In this lodge all are welcome; this lodge is open to every expression of the divine."

As I explained my position, my questioning friends softened.

"I understand," Jim concluded. After everyone agreed, we began the ceremony.

Brilliant flames danced in the fire and sent waves of intense heat into the air as the fire keeper heated the rocks for the ceremony and all of the preliminary activities were completed. I stepped into the lodge with two other women for the first round and felt the coarse hay and solid earth beneath my feet as we circled the fire pit in a clockwise procession and sat on the ground. The door keeper closed the door; the only light came from the glowing rocks in the center.

CHAPTER SEVEN

I started drumming and singing. The resonance of the drum, the smell of the sacred herbs burning, the steam, and the songs seemed completely familiar and natural to me. The welcoming song to the Creator became louder and louder, and the drum and I became one—one heartbeat.

In the darkness and heat of the lodge, streams of light swirled around the glowing rocks and myself. Soon, the whole lodge was filled with beautiful streams of light. I became aware of several spirits sitting around the sacred fire. To my great surprise and joy, I recognized the nurturing presence of Mémé. Evelyn was also there; her supportive presence told me, "You've done it! You've taken over the work."

I pondered how I—a woman born in another culture and country—would be accepted in my new function without giving up the ways of my heritage.

I prayed with deep conviction and asked the Creator to see my dilemma and give me a message. What was I to do?

Then the lodge and I were transported to another dimension, where I received a great vision. The ceiling of the lodge opened widely, and I saw planets and galaxies. In the middle of this bright summer afternoon, the universe welcomed me in a sky filled with stars and shooting lights. I saw again, as in my near-death experience many years ago, the interconnection of everything. The brilliant light I had witnessed so long ago instantly filled every atom of my body. Overwhelming love flooded me, and I wept.

The answer to my prayers pulsed in my mind as I saw a council of wizened beings sitting in a circle. "We, the elders of this land and yours, welcome you and bless you. We have seen your good intentions and have watched your deeds for a long time. Go and share what you know in your heart to be true."

When the message had been received, the vision disappeared, and I became aware of myself in the lodge sitting in front of the now darkened rocks. Mémé and Evelyn were gone now, but I felt deeply the honor they had bestowed upon me. The power and the blessing of the message I had received from the elders filled my heart, too. Tears of gratitude ran down my face and mingled with my sweat, and I could hear the other women in the lodge crying as well. Joy and gratitude had been shared by all. The first round in the new prayer house was complete.

In the days that followed the first group ceremony, I began to use the lodge as a place for my praying and singing in solitude. One morning as I was performing my daily ritual, something shimmering on the statue of Mother Mary caught my eye. I stared in amazement. Rays of sunlight illuminated the statue's eyes, which appeared to be wide open and gazing back at me.

Every day for a few minutes during my morning prayers for the next two weeks, Mary gazed at me. I knew this vision was a confirmation of the message I had received in the first lodge ceremony. I had questioned how providing a lodge would continue the work of the Bernadette Foundation. Now, I profoundly felt the presence of

Bernadette and understood that she and others spirits had guided me to create the prayer house.

One day Ken, a sundancer who had helped build the lodge, arrived to participate in a ceremony. "I brought something for the prayer house!" he beamed.

He thrust his arms outward and displayed a beautiful black bust of a powerful-looking Native American man for all to see.

"It's Chief Joseph!" Ken explained. "He led the Nez Perce people through great hardship to the border of Canada to escape persecution. When they were not allowed out of the United States, he refused to battle, saying 'I will fight no more.' He was a great man of peace."

Ken and the rest of our group reverently placed the bust of Chief Joseph in a place of honor near the statue of Mary.

"Hey! Now we have Mary and Joseph together again!" someone quipped, and we all laughed at the cosmic joke. We were sure the Creator was laughing with us, too.

Whatever befalls the earth,
       befalls the sons and daughters of the earth.
We did not weave the web of life,
       we are merely a strand in it.
Whatever we do to the web,
       we do to ourselves.

Chief Seattle

Maman Loba

Later that year, I responded to the painful cry of those living in cities, and through the Bernadette Foundation, I created another lodge. It was an urban lodge built near my husband Arthur's home in the city of Sacramento, California.

I had witnessed healing, nurturing, and individuals touching the Great Mystery in the prayer house in Mt. Shasta. Shy people had shared their most intimate selves through prayer; men had cried as they renewed relationships within the "womb of the Mother;" and Native Americans had remembered their ancestors and embraced their traditions. Within the safety of the lodge in the spirit of earth, ordinary people had seen visions, contacted spirits, and been healed. Now I was called to share the spirit of earth where it was so sorely needed.

Several months after the urban lodge was built, it received a beautiful blessing. Arthur and I had been asked to provide housing for a Huichol shaman from Mexico, Don José Benitez Sanchez, who was in the United States for an

Don José Benitez Sanchez

exhibition of his yarn paintings. Don José had started his apprenticeship as a shaman when he was only eight years old. After the death of his mentor, he became the elder of his tribe. He was now a respected leader and healer of his people, and was known worldwide for his talents as a healer and artist. During his stay, Don José blessed the lodge.

In our time together, I was constantly impressed by this great man's humility. With generosity and simplicity, he taught me ancient prayers and ceremonies he used in his healing practice. He helped in the yard as I cooked meals for him, and once he washed my car and cleaned the inside of the vehicle on his knees with a hand broom. I asked him to please stop, but he refused, saying "I want to give, too."

On the day of the blessing, Don José dressed in his tribal garments. What a marvelous sight! Ankle-length white pants were topped by a traditional white shirt emblazoned with red embroidery and tied with a fancy sash. On his head sat a straw hat decorated with a fringe of red pompons. Together we raised the colors of north, south, east, and west on the poles surrounding the lodge, and the Huichol shaman prayed in each direction.

The evening of the lodge ceremony, heavy rain fell. Huge raindrops pelted the lodge. When the final round ended and the door opened, there stood Don José! He was drenched! Water sheeted over his face and clothing. He had stood as a sentinel in front of the lodge in the pouring rain throughout the entire ceremony to maintain the sacred energy of the prayer house.

Don José greeted me warmly and hugged me with great reverence. "You and me equal," he said in his limited English. "You are a powerful healer and a great woman."

Motioning for me to wait, he quickly left and returned a few seconds later with two prayers sticks which I knew he carried everywhere for ceremonial use. Two weathered hawk feathers dangled from the end of each stick.

"I have carried these feathers for thirty-five years," Don José continued in Spanish. "Now they are yours."

He then placed one of the sticks in each of his ears. "You need José, this telephono José, Josiane!"

We embraced in the rain and my heart was filled with gratitude for the honor this Huichol shaman had bestowed upon me. From then on, Don José's gift was used in every ceremony and sweat lodge I led; the prayer sticks were placed on the altar in front of the lodge as a reminder that we were praying with him and his tribe. Each time, I felt the loving presence and support of this humorous, down-to-earth, magnificent being.

Before Don José left the United Stated he invited me to co-lead with him the harvest ceremony held every fall in his country.

Most of the work of the Bernadette Foundation was now being accomplished in the prayer house in Mt. Shasta, the urban lodge, and my office in Sacramento. People from all walks of life were coming, and each had his or her own unique and valuable experience to contribute.

CHAPTER EIGHT

Lavada was a professional psychotherapist. She came to the lodge for the health of her body and to pray for herself and others. Once she was sitting very close to me in the darkness of the lodge. I became aware of a gentle presence on the right side of her body above her shoulder. The presence seemed to be a child—a baby in need of nurturing. When Lavada's turn came to speak, everyone turned their attention to her.

"I had the most incredible experience," she began. "I was made aware of my need to nurture myself as a child, to play more and acknowledge my needs, and to feel with the innocence of a child."

Lavada was gently crying now. "How hard I have been with myself," she continued. "I have let my mind decide who I am and what I am to do."

In the lodge, I often witnessed individuals realize how their thinking or behavior was responsible for their pain, then perceive ways to improve their lives. Lavada was one such person. Terrence was another.

As many who are drawn to the lodge, Terrence was seeking healing of his addictions to alcohol and drugs. It seemed to him that religion had blamed him, and he came to the lodge in hopes of finding a spirituality more accepting of and resonant with himself. He also sought a nurturing environment, where he could feel safe enough to express all his emotions, without the pressure of behaving the way he had been taught was 'appropriate' for men. In the darkness of the lodge, I sensed the strong presence of a

Participants at a Mt. Shasta retreat.

guide next to him, and I knew he no longer felt alone. The lodge was providing a community of people who accepted, supported, and prayed for him no matter what. After the ceremony, Terrence decided to enter a rehabilitation center. He knew the task would be a difficult, but knew he would be supported through it.

Physical healing was the goal sought by Brenda. Her pale face and her shyness made her look fragile despite her strongly built body. She was environmentally sensitive, and sometimes leaving her home was impossible since she was allergic to most everything. Brenda had tried many things, including alternative medicine, but had found no relief. Someone told her that a sweat might help her, so she attended the sweat lodge ceremony. The thought of sitting upon the earth and touching dirt was unbearable to her, and the idea of sweating was repugnant! She was normally in the habit of changing her clothes several times a day. Yet the need for healing was so strong that she was ready to do whatever it took to change her life.

During Brenda's first sweat lodge, it was obvious to me how hard she was trying; her whole body fought the experience. How scared and disgusted she was at the sight of her sweaty appearance! But she returned again and again. Eventually, her attitudes toward her body and the earth changed, and with them, her health and vitality. The last time I saw Brenda, she delighted in being sweaty and dirty and feeling her renewed energy melt away the remaining resistance of her mind and body. She accepted earth and glowed with the incredible light of joy and health.

One effect of my work with the lodge was quite unexpected: Some Native American people who had not been connected with their ancestors embraced their heritage.

One day, Rebecca, a long-time student of mine, assisted at the lodge. I noticed the reverence she had for its construction, and how naturally she performed her tasks.

"What a good little Indian you make, Rebecca!" I joked.

Rebecca stopped what she was doing and turned to me. "But I am, Josiane," she replied. "I even have the papers to prove it!"

Of course it didn't make any difference to me whether she had papers or not, but I was puzzled that I had not known she belonged to the native culture of this land.

"Both of my parents are Native American," she proudly added.

"Why didn't you ever tell me?" I asked.

Rebecca's face grew serious. "Growing up as Indian was very difficult in more ways than one," she answered. "My family has very fair skin, so other Natives always mistrusted us—even when we lived on the reservation. That's why we got our papers. In the white world, we hid because of the stigma attached to Natives—drug and alcohol abusers, lazy. You know the stereotypes."

I studied Rebecca's face as I listened and tried to imagine what she felt.

CHAPTER EIGHT

"So you see," she concluded, "it has not been very easy either way."

A year after initiating the urban lodge, I was invited to attend my first Dance for Life in Washington with people of many tribes from Canada, the United States, Mexico, and elsewhere. This ceremony was similar to the traditional Native American Sun Dance—the annual tribal prayer of thanksgiving to the Great Spirit beseeching forgiveness, wisdom, peace, and harmony for all life—except that non-natives were also in attendance. I was honored to attend as a supporter of the dancers.

Upon arriving at the Dance for Life, I viewed the panorama in awe. The dance site was located on a gentle slope overlooking a village of many tepees. Fires burned brightly before the sweat lodges, and the smell of burning cedar scented the air. The haunting sound of drums greeted me. I felt as if I were walking into an ancient, primal memory.

Late the first night, after the dance's close, I was exhausted. I wearily climbed into my tent and immediately fell asleep. Sometime in the middle of the night, I awoke with a start. What was that sound? I listened intently. Wolves? Was I really hearing the howling of wolves?

All my senses were sharpened by fear. I felt their wild cries in my body. Excitement filled me as I listened to the wolves and allowed myself to receive their songs. Soon my fear subsided as I remembered hearing their calls many times in the past.

The next morning, I eagerly asked others in the camp about my experience, "What was happening with the wolf cries last night?" My companions simply stared blankly at me. "Didn't you hear them?" I asked. No one had heard the wolves but me.

The next night, I heard the wolves again, and the following morning the response was the same. I heard the wolves for three nights and was the only one to do so.

After the third night, a young woman stepped forward. "You know, Maman," she said addressing me as 'mother' since I was the elder at our camp, "maybe they were there just for you. Perhaps they are your medicine."

After that, I was called Maman Loba. That was how my medicine name meaning 'mama the wolf' came to be. I accepted the wolves as my allies.

When I left the Dance for Life, I had a great deal to consider. I had witnessed something sacred, powerful, and moving beyond words. The following week, I stayed alone and communicated with no one. I needed a week of total silence to pray and assimilate what I had experienced. I asked the Creator to please send me a sign or a vision to direct me to my next step.

In answer, I had a powerful dream. In it, I was to marry a Native American man. On the way to his home to meet his tribe, I shared with him my fear and the reasons behind my fear.

CHAPTER EIGHT

"But I'm not Indian! This is not my culture! I will be out of place," I repeated over and over.

"Trust me," my betrothed responded. "You will be welcome."

When we arrived at his village, his family welcomed me as promised with a great display of joy and colorful presents.

The marriage ceremony then began. Two women came toward me holding in their outstretched hands what looked like a necklace with a figure of a wolf at its center.

"Welcome, dear sister, you are one of us now. Have no fear of the future, for we embrace your life as you have embraced ours," they said in unison. "Soon there will be a gift coming to you in your everyday world. Then you will understand."

When I woke up, I wondered what the dream meant. Rebecca telephoned me several days later. She had been participating in the ceremonies at the lodge and now openly embraced her Black Foot and Eselen Native heritage. She was called now by her Native name: Bear Woman.

"I have a gift for you," Bear Woman told me. "I was asked in a dream last night to give it to you. My mother and I made this a long time ago," she continued, "and it has a special meaning to me. But I have been asked to give it to you. Please, come to my house this afternoon for it is not mine any longer. It is yours."

"What is it?" I asked.

"Just come to my house. You'll see," Bear Woman answered.

When I arrived at her little house that afternoon, she met me at the door dressed in her Native attire. How beautiful she looked! She embodied the true essence of her ancestors.

That afternoon, with beautiful simplicity, Bear Woman passed to me the most beautiful pipe I had ever seen. The bowl was carved into the form of a howling wolf. I burst into tears, overwhelmed by the message the pipe represented and deeply touched by Bear Woman's prayers, asking her ancestors to see my worthiness to carry the pipe in the name of her nation.

A year later, I was preparing the pipe for a blessing at the Dance for Life. I worked long into the night prior to the dance, wrapping the pipe in sage and red cloth as I prayed in a traditional way for the good of all my relations. Then I took the pipe to the Mother of the Dancers so it could be presented to the dancers to be blessed and smoked.

The following day, when I appeared at the dance grounds, I learned that my pipe had been removed by some of the local Natives; no one had been allowed to smoke it. I had not realized the resentment created by Bear Woman's gift of a pipe. I was crushed that anyone felt I was unworthy to carry the pipe. My good intentions and Bear Woman's gift of peace and wisdom had been violated.

CHAPTER EIGHT

As I left the sacred ground, I was stopped by a gentle man who, upon seeing my distress, asked me to please stay and talk with the elders, one of whom was his wife, a wonderful woman of great wisdom. We talked for a long time, and I was told to come back the next day after the council had deliberated what action to take.

Upon arriving the following day, I was told to meet immediately with the intercessor, Uncle Les, a Wasco and Yakima Native. I was filled with apprehension. I had been disgraced before everyone, and I was broken-hearted.

Uncle Les sat with his wife, Bright Star, on the sacred grounds under the arbor where he presided over the dance. I was escorted to the arbor, and Uncle Les motioned for me to sit beside him.

"I'm glad you're here," Uncle Les said, looking at me intently. "By running away, you give power to those who have offended you. Coming to face them, you have proven to be a strong warrior. You have defeated them. I'm always proud when a woman stands for what she believes. I'm proud of you."

I felt all eyes upon me.

"No one," Uncle Les continued, "has the right to take anyone's pipe. A pipe is part of your own body, like your heart, your eyes, your legs. Taking your pipe away wounds you and steals your spirit. Whoever does that to a brother or a sister will have to pay for their wrongdoing with great pain and suffering. Do not hate them for what they have done, for they are in need of great healing. Pray for them."

Uncle Les's words were like a balm to my wounded heart, but my mistrust created a visible shield of resistance. This gentle man of wisdom then held me in his arms for a time, and slowly my resistance melted.

"I have a gift for you," he said as he handed me a small pipe. "This is a much smaller pipe than the one you possessed, but it is a very powerful woman pipe which has been smoked many, many times. Look at the stem; it is dark because it has been used for a long time. Now look at the bowl; you see the constellations imprinted naturally in the stone? This is a very special pipe. Every time you smoke from now on, you will smoke not only with all your relations, but with the star people as well."

Uncle Les then called the leader of the dancers and gave him the pipe and asked his wife to escort me to the tree of life in the center of the sacred ground where I prayed for healing. As I put my arms around the tree of life where men and women had danced and given their pain, suffering, and abstinence of food and water for the benefit of Earth and all creation, a surge of energy filled my entire body. I felt dizzy. Then the haunting sound of the drums began, and the dancers surrounded me and brushed me with their eagle wings. With each touch, a new surge of energy filled me.

When the dancers were done brushing me, I was led back to the arbor. The leader of the dancers handed me the peace pipe three times. As called for by tradition, on the fourth time I received the pipe into my own hands, I was asked to face the crowd.

"This woman is not innocent any more," Uncle Les announced in a loud voice so the whole community could hear. "She now knows her duties toward all her relations."

Later, I met with Bear Woman. "I am so proud of you!" she beamed. "You are, indeed, a spiritual warrior! It took great courage for you to face the elders not knowing the outcome." Her eyes reflected a deep love which I felt in the center of myself.

"I have been challenged many times since I began my work, by Natives and non-Natives alike," I responded. "But their judgment does not affect me for too long, because I stand on the integrity of my direct experience."

"When I was in the hospital after my near-death experience, one day I watched lovers walking hand-in-hand past my window. At that moment, I promised God that if I ever walked again, I would serve Him for the rest of my life. I never dreamed that it was going to be such a long, painful, and unusual road. I have had to embrace my near-death experience for almost thirty years to assimilate its depth. There was so much more to come for its meaning to unfold—my work as a chaplain; my experiences with spirits, those seeking healing, the dying, and Native Americans; my learning in nature and the sweat lodge. These were my experiences, not anyone else's. I've learned to trust myself, my guidance, and my discoveries and allow each new experience to bring new light and wisdom."

*Maman Loba/Cedar Woman performing
a wedding ceremony.*

CHAPTER EIGHT

"What was done to you at the Dance for Life could have destroyed you," Bear Woman said, "but instead you went through an initiation. Do you see the circle that has been completed? You were brought to this country—to a new culture, to the ancestors of this land. You brought a Native American man to your country—the place of your spiritual past, your ancestors, your culture—to teach and share. You have seen the similarities."

"The 'Catinaccio' of my culture is very similiar to the 'Dance for Life' of the Native culture. In both, the suffering, blood, and sweat of participants is offered to the One Spirit for healing," I reflected, wondering how I could have foreseen my role as a bridge between cultures and dimensions. I paused before continuing and felt the warmth of the afternoon sun touching my skin and listened to the contented purr of Titou, the cat, my sweet companion of 19 years, who had joined us.

"I remember a dream I had," I continued. "In it, Evelyn spoke to me again. At the time, I didn't understand. She led me to a road which seemed to go to a part of the world I could not see. There was a bridge between the two worlds, and I could hear people on the other side but could not comprehend what they were saying. I sat in the middle of the road. Suddenly, a rainbow shot from the center of myself and extended all the way to the other side of the bridge. 'Many will come to you, and they will remember their true nature,' Evelyn said."

• • • •

For thirty years, I have dedicated my life to helping individuals to connect with their own spiritual dimension
and sacredness. My experience has taught me that there
is so much potential in each one of us, and many realities
which remain untapped because we have been made to
believe that these things are not real or are evil, or that
'special things' happen only to special people. I never felt
very special, and yet, when I look back, I realize I have
always been blessed with great gifts. I had to face death
to become aware of them. We are each special in the eyes
of the Creator, no matter what color we are, what we
believe, or what we do. We are as varied as the flowers
in the fields, and yet, each one of us is a precious part
of the great web of life.

Spirituality is not an experience; it is what we are. Spirituality is getting in touch with the natural flow of our own
lives and expressing that sacredness in our relationships,
homes, and working places. When we recognize the
miracle of life in everything, we understand our connection with the whole. Then we create a sense of wonder
in our every day lives—we create heaven on earth.

Epilogue

This is my story—the way I came to learn and trust the whispers of my soul. I lived this story, and my life continues to write new chapters filled with fresh learning, more characters, and developing new programs for the Bernadette Foundation.

I continue to hold ceremonies in the lodge in Mt. Shasta, California and the urban lodge in Sacramento, California, as well as offer private consultations, Awakening the Soul sessions, ceremonies for rites of passage, Shamanic journeys, classes, lectures, and retreats. In all the varied forms my work assumes, I offer myself as a bridge between the two sides of life so individuals may get in touch with their own guidance in the spiritual realm, feel their place in the web of life, and express the sacred within themselves in their day-to-day world.

The benefits for people drawn to my work are as unique as the people themselves. Some experience physical or emotional healing, or even the healing of a relationship with a departed loved one. Others are assisted through transitions in life or into death. Many begin conscious relationships with spirit helpers. Most learn to identify and meet their own needs, dare to express the totality of what they are, and experience the passion of their own souls.

All lives are connected as one luminous web. Everything that grows, flies, swims, walks or crawls upon the earth—every blade of grass, every person, every creature, all flowers, everything—is interconnected. As we honor and clearly express ourselves fully, we honor all life, and we ensure the legacy of heaven on earth for future generations. To this purpose, I have lived my story.

I slept,

    and dreamt that life was joy;

I awoke,

    and saw that life was service;

I acted,

    and behold: service was joy.

Rabindranath Tagore

FOR FURTHER INFORMATION
about Josiane Antonette's classes and services,
or to order additional books, contact:

The Bernadette Foundation
P.O. Box 213
Mt. Shasta, CA 96067

or visit our website at **www.mattersofspirit.com**

◆

or phone: **916/448-4348**